# BEFORE THEIR TIME

*Four Generations*
*of Teenage Mothers*

# BEFORE THEIR TIME

## Four Generations
## of Teenage Mothers

Joelle Sander

With a Foreword by Robert Coles

Harcourt Brace Jovanovich, Publishers
New York     San Diego     London

Library of Congress Cataloging-in-Publication Data
Sander, Joelle.
  Before their time : four generations of teenage mothers/Joelle
Sander.—1st ed.
    p.    cm.
  Includes bibliographical references.
  ISBN 0-15-111638-5
  1. Teenage mothers—United States—Longitudinal studies.
2. Intergenerational relations—United States.  I. Title.
HQ759.4.S25   1991
306.85'6—dc20   91-19965

Printed in the United States of America

First edition
A B C D E

For my parents,
Eleanor and Joseph Hevesi,
and for Fred, always


Side by side with the exigencies of life,
love is the great educator.

*Sigmund Freud*
*(SE,XIV, 312)*

# Contents

# *Foreword*

In the spring of 1964, a number of young civil rights activists were hard at work planning what they then called the "Mississippi Summer Project," an effort to initiate a nonviolent but vigorous and persistent political confrontation with a deeply entrenched segregation that denied even the vote to blacks, never mind access to movie theaters and restaurants and the schools attended by white children. At a particular moment, some of those youths, for understandable reasons, became apprehensive and worried—fearful of the eventual cost in lives but also perplexed about certain distinctions they had already noted between *their* objectives and purposes and those of the people they meant to reach, influence, persuade. "We are we," I heard those young men and women say—and then, after a brief pause, "They are they."

This separation, for a while, obsessed those who had given it the life of words, until, one day, a group of us went to see Dr. Martin Luther King, Jr., in order to discuss the matter with him—reflect upon the "gulf" of sorts that we believed existed between what we hoped to accomplish and what many of those who lived in the vulnerable communities of isolated and obscure Delta hamlets or towns might have in mind for themselves. Many blacks, for instance, had said a firm *no* to various voter-registration initiatives—and though fear was an obvious reason, the refusals gave us pause, maybe even prompted some fear in us: are we presuming to know what others want and need, when, in fact, they don't see things as we do and maybe even have interests and preoccupations other than ours?

Dr. King heard us out—nodding now and then, saying yes rather often but refusing us for many minutes the more extended remarks, the clarifications (and, too, the urgent exhortation, the uttered words of encouragement and sanction) we needed and sought. We began to tire, at last, of our own voices; we began to become testy, even provocative with one another. I remember the heated argument that developed: who has the "right" to speak on behalf of others, never mind take action on their behalf? Such a subject got to the heart, of course, of not only that proposed summer project in Mississippi but the entire struggle being waged at the time in the South. It was then that Dr. King spoke, and more tersely, at first, than we expected: "This [what we were discussing] is part of a larger question: who knows what about whom—who can stand up and with confidence speak the truth about someone else, about others?"

He did not immediately try to answer his rhetorical question. Nor did we. One of us murmured dissatisfaction: yes, blacks were mightily intimidated throughout the South, especially its rural sections, but the whole point of the civil rights struggle was to address such a state of affairs forthrightly. "If we start worrying about a question like that [the one Dr. King had broached]," one man insisted, "we'll lose our momentum, we'll lose our nerve, we'll lose this struggle." Dr. King saw his point, agreed—but added this comment: "In the long run, after segregationist laws have been swept aside and everyone can vote in Mississippi, we'll still be up against a lot of social problems, all over the country. People like us will want to do something about them [such problems], and we'll be wondering what to do. That's why I say we've got to understand people, first, and then analyze their problems. If we really pay attention to those we want to help; if we listen to them; if we let them tell us about themselves—how they live, what they want out of life—we'll be on much more solid ground when we start 'planning' our 'action,' our 'programs,' than if we march ahead, to our own music, and treat 'them' as if they're only meant to pay attention to us, anyway!"

I kept thinking of those words of Dr. King as I read this accessible, instructive, poignant book—a collective witness, by four women, to a family's fate over the generations and, too, a reminder on their part, to the rest of us, who have known better luck, who have had better chances, that for many women we in our abstract way regard as "teenage mothers," such an outcome can be only the latest in a series of trials and tribulations, if not outright disasters. As each of these women lets us know, to be born black and poor in America is to have, right off, a substantial burden to bear. Soon enough, the youngest of children learn the dimensions and significance of that burden; and soon enough, for all too many boys and girls, a social, an economic, a political, and not least a racial jeopardy becomes something else: an emotional and moral disintegration within the family, a disintegration prompted by sustained, severe stress. Perhaps we readily acknowledge the foregoing abstractly—even think of it with a bit more attention and concern as we watch relatively privileged people begin to fall apart in certain ways in response to a recession's unemployment, with all the attendant troubles and anxieties that accompany such an experience. But it is hard for us, no matter our goodwill, to quite fathom the circumstances of those who live at a great remove from us— their lives, their assumptions and expectations, so different from ours by virtue of their race, their class, the history of their people. No wonder Dr. King urged even his black listeners, even his fellow activists in the civil rights movement, no matter their background, to pause every once in a while, to seek out others, "to understand people first" by listening to them, learning from them—what this book splendidly enables us to do: become students, as it were, of these four fellow Americans, so that the narration of their lives, so wonderfully given us by Joelle Sander, results in the edification of our own lives—exactly the kind of "understanding" Dr. King had in mind back then as he and his compatriots tried to figure out what they ought to do, and where, and when, and in what manner.

For us, in the 1990s, Dr. King's struggle has been succeeded by one no less severe—how to work with and help strengthen millions of all too vulnerable young people, who have known, as this story's central protagonist has known, a degree of psychological turbulence that more than mirrors the larger marginality that has to do with skin color, place of residence, familial education, and income. At the end of this book, Joelle Sander, who is a talented, knowing intermediary between four narrators and us perplexed, alarmed, sometimes horrified readers, gives us plenty of suggestions, recommendations, ideas about what might (and ought to) be done. But her essay has far greater urgency and weight, I believe, because four lives have become familiar to us. We know Leticia Johnson, her mother, Denise Benjamin, her grandmother Rena Wilson, her great-grandmother Louise Eaton, in the way Dr. King urged us to know such individuals—through their lives as they themselves speak of those lives. As a consequence, we finish reading this book moved in heart and soul, even as we realize in our minds all manner of social and personal tragedies that these women, and so many others like them, have suffered over the years of our nation's history and continue to suffer even now, no matter, it seems, the power and wealth we as a nation certainly can at times mobilize (under certain conditions, on behalf of certain causes). One day, someday soon, let us hope and pray, women such as these four will also be seen as worthy of a share of that power, that wealth—and when such a time arrives, the victory will be not only theirs but ours too. We who have been privileged in so many ways will finally have become less insular, less defensively self-serving, more able to appreciate and respond to others: able to "understand" them in the way Dr. King and those who speak in this book would hope to be possible for us.

—ROBERT COLES

# *Preface*

Although much has been written on the subjects of adolescent pregnancy and parenthood, almost all of it exists in the academic literature. Interested lay readers are confined in their information to newspaper and magazine articles and to television documentaries—media that alert us almost daily to the growing problem of early childbearing but can only scratch the surface of its complexities.

What is needed is an accessible and in-depth look at teenage parenthood, not from an outsider's point of view but from those who have experienced it firsthand. No book has done this. Moreover, no book for either the academic or the lay readership has presented a full psychological and social picture of adolescent parenthood over several generations. Why, for instance, when young motherhood is so difficult, is it often repeated in this way?

In *Before Their Time*, four women in one family, over four generations, help to answer this question through their personal testimony. In the oral history tradition of Oscar Lewis, Studs Terkel, and Robert Coles, these family members make

the intricate roots of early childbearing immediate and understandable.

As a researcher and writer in the field of adolescent parenthood for the past ten years, I have followed the harrowing
path of this problem in the United States. I have studied the
increasing out-of-wedlock status of teenage mothers, the high
abortion rates among girls who become pregnant, and the
younger and younger ages at which American children become mothers. I have interviewed scores of teenage parents,
both males and females, as well as the mothers of teenage
mothers. I have listened to young people describe both their
problems as parents and the dreams they had of becoming
"better parents" than their own parents were.

As a trained family therapist and interviewer, however, I
realized that in order to go beyond a superficial understanding of adolescent childbearing, it was crucial to interview, over
an extended period of time, those who had become teenage
mothers, to break through their resistance in telling their stories, and to emerge with more than simple explanations of
their circumstances. It is my hope that these accounts of adolescent parenthood will illuminate the subject in the way
statistics and vignettes cannot, that it will offer a richer and
more complex view of both the problem and its solutions.

# *Acknowledgments*

No book makes it into the world by itself. I have many people to thank for their support and help in enabling *Before Their Time* to become a reality. Lucia and John Mudd were generous at the start in giving seed money to this project. My colleagues at Bank Street College of Education—William Hooks, James Levine, Seymour Reit, and Zina Steinberg—were consistently enthusiastic and encouraging. I am grateful for their warmth and their strong belief in this project. My thanks are also due Maryl Canon, Maureen Cunningham, and Naomi Hupert for their painstaking accuracy in transcribing the many taped interviews.

The idea for this book emerged from my work with Debra Klinman and Jacqueline Rosen on two national research and demonstration projects at Bank Street College of Education: the Teen Father Collaboration and the Adolescent Family Life Collaboration. The insights I gained from staff members at the agencies involved in these research projects and from the teenage parents and their parents whom we interviewed were critical to my knowledge of adolescent pregnancy and parenthood.

Well before this book had found a publisher, I gave readings from it. I thank Marie Prentice, Alice Olson, and Joan Marks for affording me audiences whose questions and enthusiasm spurred me on. I am particularly grateful to my friend and colleague, Alice Olson, Director of the Center for Continuing Education at Sarah Lawrence College, for her commitment to this book and for the time she gave me to finish it.

I have been fortunate in my literary agent, Susan Cohen, whose determination to see the work in print was very important to me in moments of self-doubt.

To my editor at Harcourt Brace Jovanovich, Claire Wachtel, I give many thanks for her zeal, her expertise, and her sensitivity in working with me as a partner. Many thanks also go to Ruth Greenstein, her assistant, for her gentle proddings and helpful questions and to Marge Horvitz, the copy editor, whose keen attention to the book made it finer.

Several dear friends read this manuscript at various stages: Adele Dalsimer, Henriette Klein, Kathryn Kirshner, Betsy Osha, and Marie Prentice. I am grateful to them for both their sustaining affection and for their many excellent suggestions. I am also grateful to Leon Friedman for his generous counsel.

To Karen Chase-Graubard, my old buddy, I give thanks for teaching me her ways of perseverance and imagination.

To my sons, Stephen and Jason, who never take no for an answer, I say thank you for your insistent question: "Mom, have you finished it yet?"

And to my husband, Fred, who has been my great support for thirty years, who has believed in the odd roads I have taken, whose patience and perspective mean so much to me, I am grateful.

Last, the respect I feel for the four women in this book is immeasurable. Their honesty, their courage, and their resilience inspired me throughout. Graciously, they took me into their lives and educated me. For this and for their unflagging belief that their story must be told, I thank and salute them.

# Introduction

This book is about the repetitive cycle of teenage parenthood in one family. It is a narrative of four black women: Leticia Johnson, twenty years old when I met her; her mother, Denise Benjamin, thirty-nine; her grandmother Rena Wilson, sixty-three; and her great-grandmother Louise Eaton, eighty-three. (I have changed their names, the names of other people in this book, and certain details of their lives, for reasons of privacy.) My purpose is to present their personal stories, weaving together in their own voices their memories of their childhood years, why they feel they became adolescent mothers, and the struggles they faced as young parents.

It is a striking fact that although much has been written about the great difficulties of teenage parenthood, almost no information exists about why the cycle repeats itself so often in families: why, when the children of adolescent parents have undergone the terrible problems incurred by their own parents' premature parenthood, they follow in their footsteps. Even more curious is the complete lack of personal testimony from those who have experienced this repetition firsthand, those who can provide some of the answers.

The women in this book span four generations, from the early 1900s to the present. Their accounts focus on the different eras in which they lived, the changing laws, attitudes, and social mores, and the effects these times had on their becoming young mothers. But perhaps more important, their intimate stories reveal the roots of their insistent emotional needs as young girls and the actions they took in hope of satisfying them.

I originally met these women in May 1987, through a YWCA in New York City that offered a long-standing, comprehensive program for teenage mothers. I knew of this program from research I had been doing on teenage parenthood since 1982. Specifically, I had been studying the services offered to teenage mothers and fathers and to the parents of adolescent mothers as they attempted to cope with early parenthood. During these years I interviewed many teenagers and their parents about their problems. The more I did so, the more I uncovered instances of repetition of adolescent parenthood within their families. This repetition piqued my interest. I decided to study the phenomenon of intergenerational teenage parenthood, not in many different families, but in one. I wanted to go deeper rather than broader, believing that in looking at one family's experiences in depth, I might explore its pervasive social and psychological problems. I knew, too, that I would need time to explore a family's condition fully, that the family members themselves would need time to peel back the layers of their experiences. I also believed that it would take time for them to confide in me and for me to know them.

The day I presented my idea at the Y, three girls out of the usual twelve were there. Two Hispanic girls immediately said no, they were "private people." The third, Leticia, a young black woman, her cornrowed hair streaked blond, her T-shirt reading SHIT HAPPENS, bolted out of her seat, exclaiming, "This is my lucky day! I have always wanted to write a book about my life."

Startled by her enthusiasm and wanting to believe that I had found someone as eager as I was to discuss this subject, I began asking questions about the fundamentals of Leticia's life: her age at the time of her first child's birth, where she grew up and went to school, what school was like for her. Almost immediately, however, Leticia began revealing harrowing details about her difficult life. As she spoke, I became increasingly struck by the hardened, almost rote way this young woman spoke about her experiences. Was she trying to "sell" me on her life so I would write a book about her? Were these events true? Was she demonstrating, like so many traumatized children, her need to dissociate from the pain of her past? I didn't know. What I did know was that I was both uneasy about and attracted to her macho stance. She was tough. She was articulate. She was also confident not only that she wanted to tell her story but that her mother, her grandmother, and her great-grandmother—all of whom had been teenage mothers—would want to tell theirs.

As Leticia spoke, I was both taken and moved by her extraordinary memory. She summoned up details from her earliest years. She was unafraid to remember and tremendously driven to talk about the particulars of her life.

Still, by the end of our first meeting, I was not at all sure if Leticia's enthusiastic response would be lasting. Nor, of course, was I certain that her family members would agree to participate in this project as easily as she said they would. As I left the Y, I urged her to think more about the project, which, as I saw it, would involve a year's commitment to weekly meetings. I underscored that I would be asking her many tough questions and reminded her that I wanted this to be a book not only about her own life but about the other women in her family who had been adolescent mothers. With a flick of her hand, she waved away my concerns, and we made an appointment for the following week.

Indeed, when we met again, Leticia was eager to talk.

She had also called her mother, grandmother, and great-grandmother and reported that they, too, were interested in the project.

Our second meeting went well and seemed far less frantic. Leticia was still relishing the opportunity to describe the circumstances of her life. But this time she spoke more slowly, her tough exterior vacillating between armor and a sad pensiveness. It became clear during this second interview that at least one of Leticia's purposes in working on a book was to give herself credit for "making it through" difficult times. She wanted her successes in print.

At the end of the second interview, Leticia asked me if I would pay her something if her family's story was published. I agreed to this, struck by her resourcefulness in looking out for herself and her two children (a four-year-old son and a three-month-old daughter) and cognizant of her financial need and the time she would be spending on the project.

After our second interview, I phoned Rena Wilson, Leticia's grandmother. I had learned from Leticia that this woman had been and continued to be the staunchest anchor in Leticia's life, the person she counted on for money (in addition to her welfare payments) and for practical and emotional support in raising her young children. Mrs. Wilson was sober and extremely serious. She listened to me describe the project and my own professional background and said that she would be interested in participating; that she was "concerned about the terrible epidemic of teenage pregnancy today and the fact that so little is being done about it." She added that she wanted to tell her story "so people can learn from my experiences." We made an appointment for the next week. I hardly expected that my relationship to Mrs. Wilson would become as pivotal as it did.

Two weeks after interviewing Rena Wilson, while I continued to meet with Leticia, I called Louise Eaton, Mrs. Wilson's mother and Leticia's great-grandmother. As sober as Mrs. Wilson was, Louise Eaton was funny and full of beans. She, too, was interested in the project, but because she wanted to extol the advantages of having your children young, "of coming up with them." Almost immediately in our phone conversation, she asked if I had any children. When I told her my youngest son was eighteen, she quickly wanted to know if he was married. Instinctively, I said, "Oh, no! He's too young," to which she said as spontaneously, "Mama, let your baby go!" At the end of a spirited and most amiable conversation, she invited me to her home in Queens for "the best lunch you'll ever have!"

It took longer for me to call Leticia's mother, Denise Benjamin. After several more weeks of interviewing Leticia, I reluctantly and nervously dialed Mrs. Benjamin's home. Despite Leticia's original statement that all her family members were interested, I wondered, given the particularly disturbing experiences that Leticia had described having with her mother, whether Mrs. Benjamin would be as sanguine about the project as her daughter reported. But again, Leticia had been right. Denise Benjamin was extremely friendly over the phone and was indeed eager to participate, because, as she said, "It is an important subject." After I described the project and my background, she asked me only one question: "Can I get a copy of the book when it comes out?" Her almost jovial and lighthearted tone made me uneasy about her commitment to the book. Did she realize how difficult the process of dredging up the past would be? Despite my caveats that it would require time and emotional energy on her part, she seemed eager to participate. I wondered if Leticia had told the other three women that I was going to pay Leticia if their story was published, whether they expected this too; or if they saw me as someone who could help them with some of their ongoing problems, since they knew that my past research related to services for young mothers; and/or if, like so many people who have never had opportunities to speak about their lives, they welcomed the chance to talk to someone about their experiences.

As it turned out, all of these four women wanted to talk

about their experiences; they relished the attention and the interest of an outsider. They also enjoyed the idea that a book might be written about them, although the actuality of it ultimately came as a surprise. As Leticia exclaimed when I told her that a publishing company wanted to buy their story, "Joelle, I can't believe it! When you first came to me, this was only an idea. I never thought it would actually happen!" So in part, it was their own interest in their story, as it unfolded aloud, that continued to motivate and to please them. They were putting their lives together in a way they never had before. Except for Leticia, who had been seeing a counselor regularly, they, like myself, were listening to their story for the first time.

Although I did give money to each of the four women after I signed the book contract, they had not been expecting it all along, and indeed Leticia had not told them about our conversation. It was only toward the end of my interviews, when I realized how much time I had needed to spend with each of them, that I told them I wanted to pay them for their time, commitment, and cooperation.

I had also wondered about one other aspect of writing this book. Not even knowing if I would be able to find a multigenerational family willing to take on this project, I had no racial preconceptions. I knew that I could not carry out the project with a Hispanic family, because my Spanish isn't good enough. But I had not thought about the issue of my working with a black or a white family until Leticia and her family emerged. At that point I wondered if my being white would be an obstacle. Would the color of my skin stand in the way of their confiding in me and of my being able to ask them the questions I needed to know about their lives? Would I feel like an outsider, and would they see me as one?

These questions answered themselves as time went on. I do not know, of course, what they left out of their histories, or if they would have spoken differently to a black person or to a man. Being a woman and a mother myself certainly helped me to relate to their lives. Whether it facilitated their talking to me over these three and a half years, I cannot say. I do know two things, however. Mrs. Eaton at the end of this project told me in her inimitable Southern way, "You know, da'ling, you know more about my life than anyone does." I know, too, that these four women revealed a great many difficult personal experiences to me, that over the course of my interviewing and taping them they answered hundreds of questions about their childhood years, their relationship to their parents and stepparents, the painful economic circumstances under which they grew up, their childhood dreams, their early sex lives, their work lives, and their own families' attitudes about teenage parenthood and abortion when they were adolescents. They also spoke to me about their religious upbringing and the racially motivated incidents that happened to them. They spoke of their losses, their loneliness, and their triumphs.

In the course of my interviewing, I did not restrict what they chose to talk about. Nor did I attempt to make connections for them as to why they had become teenage mothers. What developed was an ebb and flow of their memories and feelings, a dialogue between us. They wanted to talk as much as I wanted to listen. And the more we talked together, the deeper we went. These women had never been asked about their lives, nor had they, for the most part, reflected on the difficult times they endured. Like many people who experience ongoing trauma, they were far too occupied in coping with reality to ponder it. What was particularly moving was their reaction to hearing themselves speak about their lives. As Denise Benjamin said, "You know, before today, I never even thought about why I became a teenage mother."

This project began, then, in May 1987. Almost weekly for the first ten months, I went to the Y, where Leticia and I found a private room in which we could talk and I could tape our conversations. Our talks took place at noontime, but never before Leticia put away a large lunch, complete with two containers of milk. As she often said to me, "I can't talk unless I've eaten." The gusto with which Leticia devoured her enormous portions of food (and then smoked several cirgarettes) was striking. This was a hungry young woman.

On several occasions Leticia came to my apartment, alone or with her son, Terry, who left us to play or watch television. At other times I visited her, either at her great-grandmother's home in Queens, where she was staying through the summer months, or, later, in a three-room apartment in Harlem that her grandmother owned and lent her. In both places she lived with her two children.

Her Harlem apartment was neat and sparsely furnished. The living room contained two studio couches—one for her and one for her brother, Vernon (Vernon, two years Leticia's junior, moved in shortly after she had, when he needed housing)—and a small dinette set; a huge color television, the apartment's centerpiece, supported an elaborate video-cassette player. Terry and his baby sister, Hazela, slept in a small bedroom. The building, which employs a twenty-four-hour doorman, appears as an oasis of finished construction and meticulous maintenance among street after street of burned-out buildings. As Leticia said, "I feel safe here—on this side of the street."

My contacts with Denise Benjamin took place only at my apartment. She asked me in our first conversation if she could come to my home. It was clear by the tone of her voice that this had nothing to do with seeing where I lived and everything to do with her comfort in meeting away from her home. Although Denise herself never told me anything about where she lives, both Leticia and Mrs. Wilson have let me know that hers is an unsafe, drug-ridden building in which it's not unusual to see people smoking or shooting up in the hallways or stairwells. Beyond the condition of the building, Mrs. Wilson has also remarked on the messiness of her daughter's apartment. "I could never live that way," she said.

At her request, my contacts with Rena Wilson, Leticia's

grandmother, always took place where she lived. The first time, I visited the brownstone that her older daughter, Enid, rented with her husband in Harlem. Mrs. Wilson sublet an apartment on the top floor. After that, we met in the apartment that Leticia had lived in and then moved out of. I also spoke to Mrs. Wilson many times over the telephone, especially in times of Leticia's crises but also to see how she was doing in light of the increased familial responsibilities she began to take on.

Though my meetings with Louise Eaton occasionally took place at my apartment, we spoke most often in the six-room brick house in Queens that her second husband had bought in 1962, three years before he died, and that she subsequently paid off. On our first visit, Mrs. Eaton fixed a huge hot lunch for the two of us, because, as she said, "Now you're a member of the family." A fine Southern cook, she made chicken and ribs, sweet buns and rice, broccoli, cauliflower, and peas. She was disappointed when I couldn't finish the large pieces of apple pie and cake she had also made.

Mrs. Eaton's house, an hour and a half by subway and bus from Manhattan, is in a quiet, middle-class section of the borough, an area immaculately clean, with tree-lined streets and postage-stamp manicured lawns. Her home is extremely neat, despite a profusion of religious icons, knickknacks, cut-glass vases, and stuffed animals—her "children"—some twenty of which are squeezed together on her couch and chairs. There is also her "boyfriend," a large stuffed panda bear that sits on a small chair inside an unused fireplace—not to be confused with the "gentleman caller" who visits her daily and who arrived just as I left the first day I called upon her. But Mrs. Eaton's most pronounced possessions are the trophies she has won for her expertise in bridge. Hundreds of them, in all shapes and sizes, grace her entrance hall. "I am a cardplayer!" she exclaims with delight.

One may well observe that the stories in this book are about the lives of females, girls who became teenage mothers. Where

do their male partners' lives figure into this picture? Why did
they become young fathers? The partners and first husbands
in this story are for the most part no longer on the scene.
Leticia's ex-partner Terrence has some contact with Leticia's
grandmother over visiting. At some point when Leticia was
unable to care for her children, Mrs. Wilson arranged for Hazela to visit with her brother, Terry. The two families are "civil
to each other," Mrs. Wilson states, "but there's too much water
under the dam to be much more." Terrence and Leticia have
virtually no contact. Leticia's father is on crack, a fact I learned
from Leticia and her grandmother.

Despite the absence of the men's accounts, however, one
does get from these women a sense of the young men with
whom they were involved. They describe the fathers of their
children with understanding, some compassion, and an even-
handed recognition that their male partner was not the culprit in their becoming pregnant. One learns through these
women's accounts such details about the men's early lives as
their losses of their own fathers through divorce or illness,
the domestic violence these young men witnessed as boys,
and the heavy, premature responsibilities many of them
shouldered to support their families. The women did not feel
victimized by these men as much as they saw them and
themselves as having serious problems that no one could work
out. In the end, one is taken more by the similarities between
these women and their partners in becoming teenage parents
than by their differences.

A word about the structure of this book. Over the course of
my interviews with these women, I was struck by the cumu-
lative nature of their stories, the fact that with each woman's
account, I felt a stronger and deeper understanding of their
collective history: the influences of one generation on another. I decided, therefore, to re-create that same layering
quality: a weaving of the thoughts, memories, and circumstances that together tell their stories as individuals and as a
family. As I read over the manuscript, its intensity became

apparent to me. I found myself needing to take a breath not only between ideas, but also between emotions. Therefore, the reader will note that I have introduced spacing between certain paragraphs. Because I interviewed Leticia most often, in part because her life was clearly the most scarred and in part because I wanted to present to the reader the tremendous contemporary problems teenage parents face, the chapters center mainly on her.

I have divided the book into three sections. Part I contains the voices of all four women. They describe their histories—their individual childhoods through the time when they became adolescent mothers. Part II is Leticia's voice exclusively. She details her roller-coaster life from week to week, from month to month, both as an adolescent and as a young mother of two children. The dates, which span July 1987 to March 1988, include our most poignant meetings over that year. In part III, Rena Wilson and Denise Benjamin speak about Leticia's uphill battle to cope with her increasingly troubled life. They also describe their efforts and their enormous frustrations with both Leticia and New York City's bureaucracy as they try to get help for her.

The final section includes the epilogue and afterword. Here I bring the reader up to date on the adult lives of the three older women and on Leticia's current situation. I also discuss the implications of these women's testimonies in relation to the pervasive problems of adolescent pregnancy and childbearing in the United States.

And so this family's story begins. Leticia speaks first, after she has finished one of her large lunches at the Y. We sit next to each other at a long table in an empty room we have found, the tape recorder between us. Her voice is strong. Her large frame—at five feet ten inches, she weighs 170 pounds—is clothed in one of the tight jersey outfits she often wore. She wears no makeup. Her walnut-colored skin is smooth behind her large-rimmed glasses. Her cheeks are full. She is an attractive young woman of twenty.

# PART I

# Becoming Young Mothers:

## Four Voices

# 1 ▪ *"Ain't that much sorry in the world"*

---

# *Leticia Johnson*

I remember the day my parents broke up. It was the most devastating thing in my life. I remember it so clearly, as if it was yesterday or early this morning. I remember the smallest detail, even what I wore. I had on a black velvet dress with a white ruffled collar, white lace tights, and my patent-leather shoes. We was visiting my grandmother's house in the Bronx, my father's mother, Doreen. The telephone rang, and my mother answered it. It was for her. My father asked her who it was and she wouldn't tell him, so he grabbed the phone out of her hands. He spoke in the phone and then hung up. Then he hauled off and hit her in the eye. My grandfather grabbed my father, and they got into it. My father took a bottle and broke it over my grandfather's head. There was a bunch of guys at the table, playing cards. Everybody started arguing. Then my father yelled, "Where you goin'?" because my mother was getting me dressed to walk out the door. So my mother says, "I'm leavin'." I don't know if she picked up my brother, Vernon, or whether he was there. I don't even know if I was crying. But I know I seen it. I was standing on a chair watching them fight. I know my mother grabbed me and we left. I was three years old.

My parents' names are Charles Johnson and Denise Benjamin, and they can't never believe I remember this. My mother says, "Leticia, how come you recall that so good? You were so young." But I do—'cause to me, I know now, it was the end of my being close with my father.

I can't even say outright if I had any feelings about my father—whether he was around or not. I know I used to tell my mother when she spanked me, "I'm gonna tell my daddy on you." I used to say that, but I don't remember what my feelings were. Did I love him? Even now when I see him I feel so mixed.

I can't say if my father was a good father. Lately he's around more, but when I was young I saw him such a few times. Christmas and my birthday—that's about it. Put it like this— he's my father, but then he's not, 'cause he never was there. He never made hisself known to me.

   Still, I do care about him. I don't know why. I care what happens to him. But me and my father don't mix. Sometimes now I visit him in the Bronx, but I never tell him I'm coming. If he's home, he's home. We say a few words to each other. He asks me some question like "How's your brother?" and then he goes into the kitchen. He gets up and locks the door behind him. We don't talk, not about anything personal. Anyway, it doesn't bother me, 'cause we been dealing like this for a long time. But I don't know why there's such distance between us.

And my father is the kind who promises things and don't come through. He disappoints people. Like one time I was about ten years old and he promised to take me and Vernon to Great Adventure. He told my mother to have us ready that night. He was gonna pick us up. So me and my brother sat in the kitchen waiting and waiting, but he never did come. And he never did call. The next day I found out he took his other kids, from his second wife, and I was crying and crying, wondering why didn't he take us too.

And a few years ago I was working for my father—construction maintenance. I'd never do it again. When the building was built we would come in and clean behind the construction workers—take off the plaster in the bathroom, hook up the stove, plug in the refrigerator. We used to get paid fifteen dollars an apartment. But my father didn't like to pay people. So one day he gave me eleven dollars and said, "I'll give you the rest later," and I said, "Uh-uh. I want my money now. I don't care if you're my father. I want my money." And he said he didn't have it. And I told him, "Listen, this is why I didn't want to work for you." And I was warned by my grandmother, his mother. Everyone told me: "Don't work for your father, because he's no good paying people." So like a dummy, I did it because I wanted to help him and I really needed that money. So I had to quit because he never paid me. And on top of that, the week after, he asked to borrow forty dollars from me, and I said, "It'll never happen." I never ask my father or mother for no money at all. I'll go to my grandmother or my aunt.

In the times that I've seen my father, he never hit me—not once—but he always gave me the type of fear that if I do anything, he's gonna spank me. My father is tall. I think he's strong. He ain't got a lot of muscles or anything. Tall and slender. But it was his voice. He has a loud voice, and just it alone scares the daylights out of me. He always sounds mad. I can say that my father is never happy to see me. That's how I feel. He sees me when he sees me. I don't know why there is such distance between us. He knows I can take care of myself. That's why he don't bother me. But if I needed him, I don't even know if he'll be there for me, but maybe he would.

———

When my parents split, me and Vernon and my mother moved to another apartment. It was still in Harlem, in the same building as we was living, only on another floor. It's a bad building—lots of drugs and people just standing in the hallway. It's where my mother's been living for eighteen years. Two bedrooms, a living room, and a kitchen—very plain. I remember a lot of men coming in and out of our house when I was like three and four years old. My mother saw a lot of guys. Then one day, when I was still four and Vernon was two, she brought this man home and introduced him to us. His name was Reginald Carlton Benjamin. He was a big man, maybe six two, with a smooth voice. The next thing we knew, he was moving in.

Every morning when my mother went to work, she would leave us with him. Me and my brother, we would be crying our lungs out, 'cause we didn't even know this man. Then after a few months they got married. It was November 11, Veterans Day, four days before I turned five. They got married at City Hall and they had a nice reception at my grandmother Louise's house in Queens. But that day I feel my mother was taken from me. My life was invaded.

A few days after they were married, I can say it happened. I remember my brother had on his underwear and I had on my panties and undershirt. We were sitting in the living room. My stepfather told me to come over to him. Which I did. He took me on his lap and started talking to me, and that was the first day he started touching me. I was five years old. I didn't know what he was doing, and my mother never told me, "Leticia, if a man touch you in the wrong place, you let me know." She never told me that. And that's how it started. I didn't say anything, 'cause I didn't know it was wrong. But I'm not gonna lie. I know what he was doing felt good. And it went on till the time I started high school.

A few months after they got married, they sent us south. For about a year we lived in Spartanburg, South Carolina, with my stepfather's relatives. I was really petrified. I didn't know these people from Adam. I didn't know what they were going to do with us down there. All I remember was they enrolled me in some school, where I didn't do very well, and that my mother and stepfather sent us our birthday presents down there. I got Baby Alive—the doll that eats—and my brother got Evel Knievel. My stepfather's cousin started molesting me—it was just fondling. All I remember is how scared I was. I didn't know if I'd be coming home again or not, or how long I'd be staying. I didn't know if this was gonna be my family.

I was six when we came back north, and Vernon was four. I remember being so happy to be back home. But then my mother put me in a Catholic school, St. Cecilia's, which I hated 'cause it was so strict. The nuns paddled you on your hands and made you stand in the corner. And then's when I started coming closer to my stepfather. I remember I would sit on his lap when I came home from school—and he would buy me anything, whatever I needed: clothes, shoes, toys. But then I was confused too. On the one hand he was getting me what I wanted, but on the other he'd also be beating me. To this day, I feel that my stepfather threatened my mother—I don't know in which way. But if we did something she didn't like, she'd take us in the room, and my mother never beat us until she married this man. She'd make us strip completely naked and she got ironing cords, and first she'd beat us until she got tired, and then my stepfather would come in and beat us, and then afterwards he'd fondle with me. I was so mixed up.

When I think about his beating me now, it was a front for my mother, to let her think other things than "Well, I'm having sex with your daughter."

My mother pretends she has total amnesia for everything that happened to me. And I know she knows about the sexual abuse, 'cause one time I told my stepfather that I'd tell her, and all he said was, "Go ahead. She ain't gonna do nothin'." And she didn't—and she still hasn't. And that's the only thing that messes with me now, because he was right, you know.

When I think of those years, I can't figure it out. He'd be walking around the house nude, and then at night he'd get up and come into my room—start touching me when I was sleeping. If *I* was in bed with *my* husband and roll over and he's not there, I'd look around to see where he is—but my mother never got out of bed to find out. I guess she felt he was in the living room . . . whatever. But I learned to deal with it, because if that's what she wants to do, more power to her. Nothing I can do about it—that's her husband. But I tell her I wish she'd understand my side, how I feel about it. But now I come to realize that all right, it happened to me and it's not happening no more. And it's not my fault. She tells me, "Forgive and forget." I hate to say it, but I wish someday he'd drop dead, and what goes around comes around. He knows he did it. He told my mother too. And he read me this long sob story about how sorry he is. It came through one ear and out the other, 'cause it can't be un-done—it happened. That's a part of my life that will always be with me. I don't care how many times he tells me he's sorry, I'll never forgive him. Ain't that much sorry in the world.

# 2 ■ *"I didn't never want to be odd-looking"*

## Leticia Johnson

When I think about my growing up, I don't feel I had a child-hood—going outside, jump rope with the girls, hopscotch, all that, or girlfriends coming over. I never had a friend until my girlfriend in junior high. I never had a friend who comes over and you go out to the movies and roller-skate, things like that. I just never asked my mother. One time a bunch of girls from my school came to visit me at home, and my mother said I was doing my homework and I couldn't have com-pany. And they never came back again.

I don't know exactly why I didn't have friends over, but my stepfather had something to do with it. I was very shy. I was like closed. I didn't talk to many people. The whole time I was growing up, until I was in high school, I was self-con-scious about my looks. I thought I wasn't attractive to boys. And I always worried about what I wore. I didn't never want to be odd-looking or dress odd. And I was always embar-rassed because my mother bought our whole house from thrift shops, including my clothes. And when I used to go to school, everyone had on the new Pro-Keds and the jeans. And I had on these old clothes. And the girls used to say, "You have on a homemade dress." And I'd be crying all day.

Then, too, we didn't have much. Like when you're going over to a friend's house, they got a VCR, a color TV. They got a rug on the floor. They have a nice big bed. I had a plain and simple room. I didn't have a TV in my room. I didn't have a stereo. I had a pull-out couch bed and a tall, skinny dresser. I had a closet outside my room. And my room was just plain. I did have a rug, and my room was white, and that was it. And I thought that wasn't good enough for my friends to come into, and I just didn't want to invite them in.

From the time I can remember, school was a big problem. I never did like school, period, except the East Harlem Performing Arts School. I started there in third grade. My stepfather was still fondling me then—but no actual intercourse yet.

But even when I was like eight or nine, at that time, I was a problem child, so they say. I did things just to do them, without thinking. I remember once I had such a bad report card I had to forge my mother's name on it, and I didn't even give it to her. I gave it direct to the teacher. So the teacher called my mother in and said to her, "Here's Leticia's report card." My mother turned the report card over to the back and saw my signature. She looked at me with her evil look and said, "Just wait till you get home!" So that whole day I was scared, because I knew that I was gonna get a beating in the worst way, you know.

I don't remember all that happened that night, but I know when I went to school the next day my mother had beaten me so bad that even today I have the marks on my side—it was an open cut. I had one of those short tops kids wear sometimes, and you could see the marks there. And my teacher asked me what happened, and I just said, "I fell on a rock." So she put a bandage over it. When I came home from school, my mother was sitting outside with her friends. She seen the bandage, and she asked me what happened. And I called myself being smart, so I said, "That's where you beat me—I have the mark here." So she said, "You're lying. I never beat you." And all her friends was looking at her, 'cause why would a child lie like that? You know what I'm sayin'?

And I do have all the marks, even to this day, from when I had whippings and when she used to put me in hot tubs of water. I have those scars and I remember every detail about those beatings, because in my mind I won't let it die. I don't want my kids to go through the same thing. That's why I'm very skeptical about who I see and who I'm with, because I think about these things. That's the first thing that comes into my mind when it's concerning a man. I might spank my kids' hands if they do something really bad, but it won't never be to the point where they's bleeding or they can't catch their breath.

Altogether, I went to four elementary schools. St. Cecilia's and P.S. 121—those two were the pits, and I didn't stay there long. Then there was the school down South and Performing Arts, and I did pretty well at Performing Arts because I liked what we did in school with the acting and so forth. We put on certain productions, like *Li'l Abner* and *Porgy and Bess*. I enjoyed them. And we also did classwork—math, reading. And I used to play the brass bells and I played the flute. I remember that I looked forward to going to junior high school there, but I didn't get accepted so I went to another junior high, which was a good school also—the Community Learning Center. I was there for seventh and eighth grade. I did very well there. The teachers were real understanding, it seemed. They wanted us to have a good education. It wasn't like they were just there for the money. They had high expectations of us, and even though the classes were large, it didn't matter. They really put forth a lot of effort to help us learn. If there was something that we didn't understand, they'd go slow to teach us. They didn't rush through a year without us not knowing anything. I had high grades because the teachers took their time.

The problems I had was math and science. I hated both of them. And I didn't like to read just any book. The only ones I've really liked is books about the South or gangster books. My favorite ones were *Dope Fiend, Black Girls' Laws*. They're classics. *Black Girls' Laws* is about a girl who was— she was ugly in other people's eyes. She met this guy—big, husky, and real black—and they got together and got into drugs. In the end he was put in jail and she was raped, but he escaped and killed the guy that raped his girlfriend. He killed hisself and she killed herself. It was a good book, though, because it seemed so real, like everything is happening now. That's what I like—something that's real, something that's happening today that I can ID with.

But I also liked that school 'cause we had other things than academics, like a macramé class. We had a reading lab that you could choose to take, and we had arts and crafts, woodwork. I enjoyed macramé. This was like something you'd do once a day. You'd have something that you liked every day, so that also made you more willing to come to school.

In junior high once, my grades were so good that the Urban Coalition League picked me and a couple students out of the New York City schools—from all the five boroughs—to come together. We took a trip to the Poconos for a weekend. We talked about how we could better ourselfs and our education. It was nice. We had parties at night. We had cabins. We went hiking. But I got in trouble. I had went off on Saturday night to the cabins when we were meant to stay in the big dorm. Two other girls and me, we had went off with these other guys. But we were just in the cabin talking about other schools.

It wasn't like we were doing anything, because we weren't. But the teacher that brought us, she found out that I was in this cabin with these guys, and she thought the wrong thing. So she told my mother when I got home, and I got into real trouble. I was supposed to go on my eighth-grade trip, a camping trip, and I didn't go. The school didn't stop me, but my mother did.

And then also the embarrassing thing about it was I had gotten my menstrual, and my stepfather—I don't know how to say this—my stepfather had my pants. You know when you get a spot. So he said, "What's this? What was you doing?" So I was like, "I wasn't doing anything. It's that time of the month." So he showed it to my mother and he says, "Yeah, she was doing something—she came back with grass stains on her pants." And I wasn't in the grass. We all went hiking.

I know my mother didn't trust me then, I guess because she knew I was the age where I might try, but I never thought like that. I never went out with a boy until I got to high school. I didn't feel comfortable being with any boy, because my stepfather was having intercourse with me.

I always think maybe now my mother may understand that some of the things she did was wrong, but she doesn't say she does. Sometimes my grandmother tells me that my mother may have inherited a mental problem from her father. There were times she did seem crazy to me. Maybe that's true. I don't know. I don't know what to make about her actions. I know she wasn't taking no drugs, and she didn't drink, 'cause it was against her religion, so maybe she was crazy.

The hard part is now when my mother says to me, "I don't understand why you and your brother have such resentment toward me. I raised you properly, and I don't see why Vernon acts the way he does." And I tell her, "I know why he does." But I don't tell her I know it's because of the way she treated him, the way she treated me. I had a lot of resentment for her too, but I outgrew it. They gave him the same punishment they gave me, but rougher because he's a boy. My stepfather used to hit him with a stick—whatever he could find. Now he doesn't associate with them. Vernon dropped out of school to work when he was sixteen, and he's been taking care of hisself for three years. But my mother, she keeps saying, "I don't know, I never did anything to you all." But I know different, because I have the bruises and the pains to show for it.

After junior high I went to Norman Thomas High School. I didn't even choose that school. I choosed Music and Art and Art and Design and the ABC [A Better Chance] program, which is a go-away program. You go away and stay for the full four years. You live on campus either in a city or like in the South—wherever you want to go if you're accepted into the school you apply at. But I never got accepted. You have to take a test. I guess I didn't pass . . . whatever. I didn't get into Music and Art or Art and Design, but I did get accepted to Norman Thomas, which at that time was a very good school. I was thirteen going on fourteen the year I started high school.

I remember when I first started going, everything was pretty good in school, but things at home wasn't. My mother and I was really at it—arguing all the time. She had become a Jehovah's Witness when I was around six, and she was too strict. I never had any freedom to go anywhere besides school–home, school–home. I couldn't go to the movies or parties. I never was able to do anything. And I was feeling bad about my body. I remember 'cause the kids were talking about sex and I used to think, Wait a minute, this is what's happening to me at home. And I really felt it was my fault. I used to cry at night and think, This is my fault, why am I doing this to myself? And I didn't know. Then, parts of my body, I just thought was bad. I said, Why do I have to have a vagina and breasts? Why?

———

It was that October of my freshman year that I met Terrence, my kids' father. All I seen was just me and him. Everything else was blurry. He was the first boyfriend I ever had, and I was so excited. I remember coming home from school about a few months after I started seeing him, telling my mother about this boy, and she said, "Leticia, you can't see no boys unless you're ready for marriage—you know what our religion says." I didn't care nothing about no Jehovah's Witness. And besides, the way they practice their religion scared me to death. Some of the things are similar to Catholic teachings, but when they found out that I was having intercourse with Terrence. . . . My mother wasn't even sure I was. She just assumed it, and she told the Brothers to come and talk to me. I thought they was doing some kind of voodoo on me or something. They say like "People of the World"—everybody who's not in their religion is "worldly." They got me scared, you know: "worldly"—they make you seem like you's a devil. And like now, I'm so afraid to go to church, even just to sit there or go to confession.

And my stepfather didn't want me to see Terrence either. And it was hard on me. I mean here's a boy that I really like, and he was turning him away from me. Why? I felt good when I met him, and my stepfather tried to take that away from me. I was feeling self-conscious about my body then, about my looks, and I know it had to do with the sexual-abuse stuff. I felt ugly. And then, also, when I first started high school I like wanted to blend in. The girls and guys, you know, they dress in a certain way, and being a freshman, you have to fit in with the crowd. I didn't never want to look different. And I'd come home from school and say, "Mama, you just gotta get me this. I'm not going to school if I don't get it." And she wouldn't get it for me, but my stepfather, he'd be buying me the stuff and I'd be takin' it, you know.

When I met Terrence I fell in love. I can say that nothing else mattered to me. I didn't care what my mother said. I used to talk back to my mother, and I wanted to be with him every day—every minute! That's when I started being myself. And I'd see him all the time in school. We both went to Norman Thomas. He was fifteen when we met. We're about a year apart.

At first we started cutting classes to be together. We got real close. I felt he was like a protection to me. I knew he'd come to my aid whenever I needed him—like Romeo and Juliet. At times, if I'd go to school and I didn't come straight home after, I'd ask him to come home with me 'cause I knew my mother was going to beat me. But then when he did, my mother'd be handing him these books about youth. She'd be saying, "You shouldn't be going out with each other unless you're ready to get married." I was just fourteen, so why was she telling him all this? I couldn't understand why my mother didn't want me to be with him. I was thinking, Why are these people telling me that I shouldn't see him and I shouldn't do this, if my own stepfather who lives in my home is doing things to me? They didn't understand that being that I was home and this was happening to me, I needed the same comfortable feeling from another man. That's what I missed.

I really disliked my mother for this, not seeing my view. Why would she want to try and hurt me, do something to disturb my life? One night, I remember being so mad at her for telling Terrence the Jehovah's Witness stuff, I just ran away. He couldn't find me for a few hours. Finally he was upstairs at my house and I was standing in front of my building. He saw me and came down to talk to me. He tried to tell me to come back upstairs, but I was like, "No! I'm gonna get out of here. I don't want to stay." And he had been talking to my stepfather, so he said, "I don't see what's wrong. You've got nice parents." And I was like, "You just don't know what I've been through." I was afraid to tell him. So he said that maybe

I could stay there for a while and then ask my grandmother to tell them that I wanted to live with her. So that's what I did. But she said, "I don't think that's a good idea. I think you should stay home and try to cope with what's going on." But my grandmother didn't exactly know what was happening, because I didn't tell her yet. Though she did sense something was wrong.

It's hard to describe how I felt about Terrence. He was my whole life. He was all I could think about. We was real close. There was many times when I was home, and my mother never celebrated Christmas or Thanksgiving or birthdays, and Terrence would give me a gift. He'd give me fifty dollars on my birthday, and that was November, and then right after, when Christmas would come, he gave me twenty-five dollars, and I told him I couldn't accept it, because my parents don't celebrate. And he was like, "I'm not taking it back. It's yours, you can do with it whatever you want." So I had to hide it. And one time I hid it under my bed and my stepfather came into the room to turn my bed over, to air it out, 'cause I used to wet my bed till I was seventeen. And he found the money, and he wanted to know where I got it, so I told him, "My boyfriend gave it to me." So he was like, "Well, you're not getting this money back." I should have put it underneath my rug—that would have been the best place. But I tell him now, "You owe me ten dollars."

Terrence was the first person outside my mother I told about what happened to me. One day I remember we was standing at the train station, laughing about things, and I just said right out, "Terrence, my stepfather is having sex with me." And he laughed, and I said, "What are you laughing for?" My facial expression just changed completely. First I was laughing, until he started laughing at me. Then I got angry and I said, "What's so funny?" And he said, "He would never do anything like that to you. He's nice." And I said, "That's what you think, but you don't live in the same house with me."

After I met Terrence, you never would know I was shy. All this changed. Everything was new for me. I started being open. And I had this kind of outlook on life, we both did, that we were gonna live together, we were gonna have everything, we would never leave each other. I used to always dream like that, even before I met him, that one day I would meet a nice man, get married and have kids, and I'd never have to come back home again.

But the whole time Terrence and me was together, my mother was trying to keep real strict about us. I never had any freedom. I remember one Valentine's Day, I wanted to go to the Valentine's party that the school had, a dance, and I begged my mother. I called him and told him I was still trying to get her to let me go, and I begged and begged and she said no. So my mother and stepfather went out shopping, and while they were out I tried to commit suicide. I took a whole bottle of aspirin. When my stepfather came back, I heard him coming in the door. I was lying on the couch, and I just fell out. I remember they was trying to get me up, but they couldn't. And I just kinda blurred and said, "Ma, I took a whole bottle of aspirin." And she said, "Why?" And I told her, "You won't let me go to this party, and I'm killin' myself." I told her, "I don't want to be in this family. I don't want to be a part of nobody here." And I know she felt bad.

They took me to the hospital, and I remember they gave me something black to drink, and this yellow stuff. It was disgusting, and it made me puke. I felt so dizzy. And she told Terrence what I did.

After that, he and me, we just started cutting school so much, I hardly went at all. My mother'd get these cut letters. One day I remember, when she got a letter I was in my room, and she came up behind me and she asked me, "What's these letters for? Why are you stayin' out of school?" And I told her it was none of her business. So she slapped me, and we got into a fistfight. I was still seeing Terrence, and I wasn't gonna let nothing she said stop me—even though that was my mother, I still was gonna be with him.

In May my mother discharged me from school and sent me down South. She told me, "Pack your bags. We're goin' away." This was almost near the end of the school year, and even though I hadn't been doing too great, I feel at least I could have tried. But I was facing a lot of problems, living at home and having to sneak to see him.

My mother took me down South to my stepfather's relatives and then left me there by myself. She was supposed to put me in school down there, but she didn't. She just left me there. But my trip didn't last long, because they are also Jehovah's Witnesses. They're deeply involved in the religion, so I used my head and got back home! I wrote to Terrence every day, made calls on their phone. They started getting tired of me. Then when my stepfather's niece Margaret would ask me, "What do you all do up North?" I'd say, "Oh, girl, I be hangin' out, goin' to parties, stayin' out to all hours of the night. We be gettin' high, shootin' some needles, dope, sniffin' cocaine." And after we'd finished talking, it seemed like everything would get real quiet. The next thing I knew, I'm sitting there looking out the window, and Margaret says, "Aunt May wants to talk to you." So I went to see what she wanted, and she just said, "Leticia, start getting your bags together. You're going back home." You should have seen the expression on my face. I was so happy! I called Terrence and told him to meet me at Penn Station. "I'm takin' the Amtrak home!"

That evening, my grandmother came over and wanted to know why my mother sent me away in the first place. So my mother told her about me cutting classes, and my grandmother said, "I'm taking her," and I told them, "I'm going." And I've never been back since. I was fifteen years old.

# 3 ▪ *"I was saying to myself, 'Why can't I get pregnant?'"*

## *Leticia Johnson*

When I got back from down South, I migrated everywhere. I never stay in one place. First I moved into my grandmother Rena's house and then to my aunt Enid's, my mother's older sister's. She lives in a brownstone in Harlem with her husband, James, and her daughter, Maureen, who was eleven then. There was much more room there, and I had the basement to myself. I could have company over, I didn't have to be in at a certain time. And my aunt used to take me shopping, buy me clothes, everything. But I guess because I wanted to be with Terrence so bad, I rebelled—I didn't listen to nobody. Everybody there kept telling me, "Go see other guys, don't get involved with one. Expand your horizons," they used to say. And I didn't want to listen. I just wanted to be with him. So I ran away from my aunt's and went to live with Terrence's sister, Rita. My grandmother and my aunt found out where I was, though, and came and got me. Then I moved back with my grandmother and her husband, Elias, again, because my aunt didn't want me back after what happened. She was disappointed with me because I ran away and, too, because she was really helping me, doing things for me, and I kinda took advantage of her.

Then my grandmother got me a job at McDonald's, and I was working—I was out of school because I was still discharged. But one night I decided to go out with Terrence and I stayed out real late. When I came home, Elias had gotten drunk. God bless the day! I guess after them telling me so many times to come home at a certain time, he got mad and cursed me out. He told me to leave. My grandmother and him got into a big fight because she didn't want me to go. But I called Terrence and told him, "Listen, my grandfather kicked me out. Can I come stay at your house for the night?" And his mother said yes, so I ended up moving in.

I started tenth grade when I was living with Terrence and his mother and his stepfather, and I remember everything was so beautiful. I was so happy. I cooked, I cleaned. I loved it. In school, I had this friend named Benita Justin, who I really liked. Then one day she told me, "Guess what—I'm pregnant." And I was real happy for her. But before she even told me, I was thinking I wanted a baby with Terrence. So I was glad for her, but then I was also kinda upset. I was saying to myself, What's wrong with me? Why can't I get pregnant? And I felt—how can I explain it?—like something was missing. Something was missing in my life. And it seemed like everybody around me was pregnant in school or already had their babies and was still attending, and I remember thinking at the time, Well, this is what's in—having a baby.

Then in October, two months after I moved in with Terrence, I found out I was pregnant. At first I was real glad, but then things just seemed to go downhill. Terrence's mother was real mad. She said, "Well, you're young, why don't you have an abortion? You don't know how to handle a baby. You'll have all sorts of problems." And the girls in school, once I was showing, started drifting away. I didn't expect that. Maybe they just thought that I couldn't have fun with them anymore, that I couldn't hang out with them, but anyhow the fun I was having just stopped.

My grandmother was the first person I told. She took me to get my pregnancy test, and when I found out I was pregnant, she actually told me to get an abortion. And I said, "No." Then I waited like four months until I told my mother. She was still a Jehovah's Witness, and she said, "You know I'm not for abortion, and I really wish you hadn't gotten pregnant, but all I can tell you is to do the best you can to take care of that child." And I waited seven months till I told my father. He was very disappointed. "Have an abortion," he said. "You can't take care of it." And I was like, "No, you're another one I can't talk to." And he said something that really made me mad, and because he still says it. "If you hadn't laid down and opened your legs, you wouldn't be pregnant now." But I told him, "Look at you—you was eighteen when my mother got pregnant. How are you gonna get on my case about having a baby?" It's like life repeats itself, you know?

But nobody was really mad at me. That's what I think. They could understand . . . well, maybe more my grandmother. And I couldn't care less if my mother and my father understood. I think my grandmother understood how girls think—you have the baby, someone to love, someone who'll love you, someone to talk to. This was going to be my child. Nobody could ever take him away from me. So I made my decision to have my baby.

But then I started feeling depressed. I was getting this big belly. I felt ugly. I didn't want to go nowhere. So I dropped out of school. I was sixteen. And then, you know, I was upset. Before I got pregnant, Terrence and I talked about getting married. I always told him, "I don't want to be like my mother, I want to stay with my kids' father." And we were supposed to get married, until his mother talked him out of it. And we were gonna stay together forever. This was me and his idea: we was gonna raise our kids, he was gonna work, and I was gonna take care of the kids and help around the house. But he is very close to his mother. He's the only boy—he has three older sisters—so he listens to her, and in her eyes he can't do nothing wrong.

But there was a lot wrong. We used to get into these fights, and for a while I'd be going to school with black eyes and rings around my neck—he tried to strangle me because I wouldn't listen to him. And I'm like . . . my own father has never, in my twenty years, put a hand on me, and I told him, I says, "You're not my father, you know. You have no rights puttin' your hands on me." Even if I was married to him, he'd have no rights like that.

And his mother would condone it. One time, when I was pregnant with Terry, we got into a argument and he had punched me in my stomach and I was sittin' behind the door, cramped up, and I was screamin', and his mother came and said, "Stop that screamin'! Whatcha screamin' about? Get up! I'm trying to sleep." And I said, "I was screamin' because I was trying to get you up so you'd help me." But she didn't do nothin'. And I really think that Terrence got this physical-abuse stuff from his father. He used to beat up his mother. He was a alcoholic, but he left when Terrence was about twelve, and then he died of a heart attack when Terrence was seventeen. His mother was already living with his stepfather for a few years. I don't think they're married. But maybe it's common-law.

Then, too, I can say that I kinda forced Terrence into having a child. Just before I had gotten pregnant, we sat down and talked about having a baby, and he was like, "Right now I'm not ready to because I have so much going for me. I'm working and you're still in school. Why don't we wait?" So I was like, "Terrence, I really want to have a baby. You don't even have to take care of it. I'll do all the work." He was like, "You sure?" And I said, "I'm sure." And he said, "Well, I'll tell you right now I'll give you the money, as much as you need to take care of this baby, but I ain't gonna be changing no diapers. I'm not gonna be sitting up late." So I agreed. I stopped taking my pills, and I found out I got pregnant around October 10. October 17 is Terrence's own birthday.

I gave birth to Terry in June, and a lot of things started happening. At first I was real excited. I was happy knowing that I'd have someone to raise who would always be with me. When Terry was an infant, I used to sit and talk to him. I knew he didn't understand, but I would tell him when I was mad, "You know, Terry, I'm so sick of so-and-so," and he'd just sit there and smile, and I'd end up laughing and not being mad anymore. He was good company. Only thing was the getting up in the middle of the night, feeding him every three hours. That was hard, and I really never got used to it. I don't think anybody does.

But then when Terry was a few months old, me and Terrence started going out with other people. And we used to have fights about that. He would lay his wallet down and go take a shower, and I'd look in it. I found all these girls' numbers, and I'd write them down and put them back. Then when he'd leave I'd call them up. I'd just listen to their voice or ask who they were, like I'm the telephone company. Then when he'd come home, I'd say, "Terrence, who's Barbara?" "Oh, she's just a friend," he'd say, but then she'd start calling the house. He'd try to cover it up, until one day he told me.

He used to go out every weekend, and I would take his keys to prevent him from going. And he used to ask me, "Where's my keys?" and I wouldn't tell him so we'd be fighting and I'd give him his keys and he'd go away. Finally I stopped doing that. I done it a lot of times, and maybe I did it because I used to like being beat. What I'm saying, 'cause I did it so much and I knew what'd happen.

The only time I ever fought him back physically was once when he was down in the basement taking the tags off these coats, and I came down and saw them and I wanted to know who were these coats for. So he told me it was none of my business—to leave him alone. So finally I went and got the table leg—a broken piece of a table—and he wouldn't tell me, so I bashed him upside his head. Then he told me they was my Christmas presents, and I told him I thought it was for that girl. When we went upstairs, his mother said, "What happened to you, Terrence?" So I said, "I'm sorry, it was an accident." And she said, "It wasn't no accident. You meant to do it." And I said, "Yes, yes, I did. I'm tired of him hitting on me." But his mother never asked about *his* hitting me. She just took his side. He could go rob a bank and he'd be all right. She'd say, "No problem." They coddle, pet him, you know, and that's bad.

But I was seeing other people too. Truthfully, I don't know who was seeing somebody else first. But I started seeing a number of men. It was only an intimate thing, sexual. It wasn't nothing like starting a relationship with someone. And I felt, too, that being sexually abused had something to do with me seeing so many guys. I don't know exactly, but I feel . . . if, say, for instance, it didn't happen to me, maybe I might not have been so quick to jump in the sack with the first person I seen. I would have been a little more cautious. I wasn't scared of sex. I wanted it more and more. I was seeing like maybe five guys at one time, plus Terrence. I can confide in males more than females, and even though I couldn't talk to my father, I needed that fatherly image. And it was hard to find . . . and I tried to get it from every guy I could.

# 4 ▪ *"If the school knew, you had to leave"*

## Denise Benjamin

*From the time we first met, at my apartment, Denise Benjamin was cheerful and chatty. She put us on a first-name basis immediately. Full-bosomed, full-hipped, almost as tall as her daughter, she looks very much like Leticia. She has the same brown eyes, round cheeks, and walnut-colored skin. She, too, wears large-rimmed glasses. Denise laughs and smiles readily but gives the impression of being at once lighthearted and guarded. Although she, like Leticia, seemed to want to speak about her early years, she was more cautious at first about revealing the events of her adult life.*

*Denise Benjamin shares her daughter's voracious appetite. At each of our interviews—except for the last, when she was under doctor's orders to lose weight—she relished a large second piece of cake.*

*Interviews with Denise went by quickly. I suspect that part of the reason for this was her obvious curiosity in thinking about and describing the many details of her life. From time to time, she was visibly surprised that she had not talked about a subject before, not made connections she was now making as she entered her forties.*

When I got pregnant with Leticia, I was a senior at William Howard Taft High School. I was a big teenager, five feet eight and heavy like now, so thank God no one could tell. I knew one other girl who was pregnant, Julia Burton. At that time— Leticia was born in '66—it was very hush-hush, taboo. If the school knew, you had to leave. Go to night school. But I was so near graduation and I wanted to try to finish and my girl-friend did too, so we knew each other's secret, but we never told. When I graduated I was four months pregnant.

Today it's so different for kids. More liberal. I mean it's still rough for a girl with a baby, but if it should happen, God forbid, they can still stay in school. They can still complete. Today they're not ostracized by their peers or the community.
But then, on the other hand, when I look at these girls I feel they lack the family support I had when I was a young mother. Families have broken down. So many are in real distress. No money. No husbands. No hope, really. And the young people I speak to are dropping out. They're afraid of the violence, the whole drug scene. They're afraid to go to school, that they're going to be physically hurt. This wasn't true in my time. You weren't afraid you'd be assaulted!

Until this day, I never really sat down and thought about why I got pregnant. I guess it was a passionate moment. And I think, too, at that time they just didn't talk about the facts of life, like we do now. It wasn't that I was naive. I was knowledgeable about what could happen, but Charles and I were in the heat of passion, and we were young. When we met, we were both seventeen.

And, too, my idea of contraception wasn't very good. I thought I knew about it, and I thought I was using it, but I wasn't. Norforms. I don't know where I got this idea, or if it was like some girl talk or what. I don't even know if they make them anymore. It's like a suppository, and it's supposed to cleanse a woman internally. And while I know that now, I thought it was a birth control. But it wasn't. So I was just adding fuel to the fire. But I think it was maybe just once or twice or so in the heat of passion that we had sexual relations, and I got pregnant.

And you know, you didn't have the big campaign you have now about contraception. Like I was telling Leticia, if I wanted information about birth control—say I thought I was gonna have sex—I couldn't just walk into Mount Sinai Hospital and say, "I'd like to go to Planned Parenthood." There was nothing—and if there was, I wasn't familiar with it. Nobody talked about such things in school. And I went to a Catholic school, and they dared not, for sure. I mean you didn't even use the word "pregnant." You said, "She's in the family way."

It was such a different time. I try to tell Leticia now, "You know, when I went to the doctor for the first time, it was when I got pregnant with you." My sister, Enid, took me. My sister's a nurse. I was just about a married woman. And she says, "Mommy, things were so archaic then." But it was just such a different time for me than for her now. And I feel I was pretty sheltered from a lot of things, you know. I never went alone to a doctor until I started going for prenatal care. And that makes a big difference in what you know about things, about taking care of yourself.

But my pregnancy wasn't like a thing of just wild abandon. We had sat down, Charles and me. We had talked about getting married. We didn't plan the pregnancy, but we did plan the marriage. But then I found out I was pregnant and I felt that I would go ahead with it. I didn't want an abortion. And I was happy.

When I told my mother about my pregnancy, though, she was very upset. She did present me with different options. She suggested I could get an abortion, but she never forced me. And anyway it was illegal, though people did get them. But my mother has always been a hardworking parent, sometimes working two jobs, so it was a real blow for her. Being a civil servant, she had always suggested that I could take beginning office work or civil service when I graduated. She had said, "When you have a family of children, you can't just live off love, Denise. Love doesn't pay the bills." My mother's very realistic. A very practical person. So she did sit Charles and me down when I got pregnant and tried to help us to see the reality. But I know I still tended to fantasize about having a baby—having a family, really. I always wanted six children and a nice little house, you know. Even though I told her, "Yes, I'm sure I can handle a child," I had this dream of a picture-perfect marriage—that Charles and I would go places and travel, and I'd bring him his slippers—the kind of thing you saw on TV in those days.

And, too, marriage was the one big goal! A lot of my friends were talking about getting married, though most of them got married after high school. And besides, I never really thought about going to college or what I would be. And my father was a disabled veteran, and the VA told me they would send me to school. But you know, it wasn't until much later that I even thought about the fact that I didn't think of going to college. Because I was a very good student. I made high grades, and I could have gone. And maybe part of it was that our school college person never even asked me. And she would ask other girls where they were going. And I don't know if it was because I was black or what, but she never did ask. I wondered much later why I never approached her. Why didn't I ask her why she didn't talk to me about college? But in some ways I know I wasn't really thinking about careers, even though other people were thinking about them for me.

When I think back too, my mother was always a career woman. She was the provider of our family, but I used to imagine when I had my children, I'd like to be there for them a little more than my mother could be there for us. I wanted to take care of them. I was what they call now a latchkey child. I would come home from school and be by myself. Even before I went to high school, I was alone after school because my sister was six years older and she was already working. And I remember it was very lonely. My mother would always call me and see that I was all right, and she'd tell me to do my homework, but still it was hard sometimes. I'd be sitting at the window watching the other kids, and I just wanted to be there with them. But I was supposed to stay in my house, and I was responsible for myself.

Charles and I, we didn't think through the financial aspect of marriage and children. All I thought was that I'm gonna be there for my kids. But then that involves cash. I didn't antici- pate we couldn't pay the rent or that Charles would get sick. Two weeks after we got married, he started to have muscle spasms, so there were periods of time he was out of work. Flat on his back. We had to go on public assistance.

When I think about it now, Charles and I were so young. He had just dropped out of high school in the eleventh grade. He was the oldest of seven brothers and sisters. Charles tried to help his family, but his mother and father didn't get along well. They had a lot of domestic problems. His father drank and he was kinda abusive.

I think, being the oldest, Charles beared the brunt of it. He tried to protect his mother, and sometimes his father would go out and he wouldn't bring money home, and I think that's one of the reasons why he was so, you know, helpful. He tried to work, and "Here, Mom, here's twenty dollars for dinner," like that. He was a very responsible person, a good person. I remember his parents weren't 100 percent about our getting married, but I think they felt he was responsible enough that if this was what he really wanted to do, then OK. He was still young, but he was working. More or less he was taking care of himself.

Sometimes I sit down and I tell the kids, "Your father and I, we loved each other at that time. The main thing was we were just too young." We couldn't cope with a lot of the stresses of early marriage. For one thing, Charles and I, we couldn't commit to one person. I had another relationship, which I don't think Charles ever forgave me for. Then he had one—it was tit for tat. And that had a lot to do with our problems. We started having physical fights. He couldn't trust me, then I couldn't trust him. I think we had Vernon to prove we were still close, that we could get close again, but we couldn't. Finally we had our last big fight and we separated—for our sanity. We were twenty-one. Leticia was three years old and Vernon was a little over a year.

It's a sad thing. You always think you're gonna be different from your parents. Do it differently. It's really a hopeful thing at the beginning. But we were too idealistic. I just thought if I only had a husband, everything would be fine.

I think about when I first met Charles, how I liked him right away. He seemed so mature, not silly like other boys. He was capable. I didn't know that kind of a man in my life. My father wasn't available to me when I was growing up till maybe when I was fourteen or fifteen. He had a nervous breakdown a short while after he got out of the army. And at that time, when a person had a breakdown of that sort, they were put in the hospital for a long time. He stayed in for eleven years. I was about three when my father went in, and I can still vaguely hear my mother and grandmother Louise talking about "William in the hospital." William James is my father's name. These words are still in my mind.

I remember so well visiting my father at the hospital when I was a young child. My mother would drive us there—out to Kings Park, Long Island. It's not that far, actually—maybe an hour-and-a-half drive—but for a little girl, it seemed to take such a long time. I could never go into the hospital. I remember my mother would go in and I'd sit in the car, and then she'd get me and I would stand by the car, waving at him at his window.

I don't ever remember seeing my father close up. When I was young he was always at a distance. I never hugged him or said "Hi." I never had that physical closeness. But my father would write me and send me books—the classics: *Robinson Crusoe, Little Women, The Bobbsey Twins at the Seashore, Annie Oakley.* And I know that's where I got my love for reading. And he would always send along a little letter. "How are you?" Never long or anything, but enough to let me know he was thinking of me. I don't remember seeing him much as I started getting like nine, ten, eleven, but I remember maybe five, six, and seven.

I know I felt very confused. My mother tried to explain to me that he was ill, and I understood that much, but she never explained in detail. I was confused why he was in the hospital so long. I thought it must be a really bad sickness. I can remember I was happy that he sent me the books and things, that we had a type of relationship, but it wasn't until I actually went to see him that I got a better understanding of what exactly was wrong.

When I was about fourteen, he was released, but my mother and father never got back together. He went to Missouri to stay with his family, and I visited him when I was about fifteen. I flew out there for a summer and stayed with him and my grandmother. He was only able to function a little. From what I remember, he seemed very childlike. He could work for short periods, but then he'd stop because he was so nervous. Sometimes we would talk but just a sentence or two— no real conversation.

When I came back to New York, I started high school. And I was having a lot of problems. I had gone from a small Catholic school to Washington Irving, which is eleven stories high. I felt overwhelmed, like I was being shuttled around. Also the freedoms of a big school were completely new to me, and I just went wild. For six months I was in with a bad crowd of girls and I was out of control with boys. I wanted to go out all the time.

A lot of things were starting to bother me. Especially how I didn't know my father. So I said to my mother that I wanted a chance to be with him more. And she said, "Well, maybe you should give it a try—see how you like it." If I remember, the VA sponsored my trip out there, because my father had some money put up for me. So I went back out to see him that summer and I stayed for a year.

By that time, my father was more like an everyday person. He wasn't as childish as he seemed to be the first time. He was able to work, he had a job, and he . . . but how can I say . . . ? He wasn't the type of person who'd come and say, "Let me see your homework," and stuff like that. I don't know what kind of relationship we had. What would you call it? He would say, "How are you feeling?" He was very caring, but . . . I don't know. He probably didn't know how. That's probably what it was. After all those years away in the hospital, he never learned how to be a father. Still, I think it helped me to see him, because I had no conception of a man. I never grew up with a man around.

At the end of the year I moved back to New York. Gramma was very old-fashioned, and I liked boys. I wanted them to take me out and things, and she said, "No. You're under my care." And my grandmother wasn't one to bite her tongue. "If you don't like what I'm doing, the best thing is to go back to New York." So that's what I decided. I was so used to being on my own. I just couldn't understand at the time that she was looking out for my interests. I didn't feel that at all.

When I came back, I started William Howard Taft High School, which was a smaller school than my first high school.

I started going out with boys much more then. We went around in groups a lot. We'd go to the movies. Nothing very private, though. We just hung around as friends for the most part. Then in that year I met Charles, about a year after I left my father.

# 5 ▪ *"I got my own place"*

## Leticia Johnson

Altogether, I lived with Terrence about two and a half years. He graduated high school during then and got a job at Woolworth's when I was pregnant. But he used to tell me, "I hate this job, I gotta sweep, I have to clean, and I'm only getting $3.35 an hour." So I told him get another one, which he did. He saw an ad in the paper to help build U.S. battleships, so he got that job and he was bringing home more money and his attitude seemed to be better. And let me not lie: Terrence was never stingy with his money. He used to give it to me all the time. I was very spoiled by him. He used to give me anything I wanted. It was just that we couldn't get along. Anywhere I wanted to go, the money was there. He'd keep it up in his closet in a little box. I'd take it and I'd go. And all's he said sometimes was, "Where's all my money?" and I'd tell him I spent it. And he'd get mad, but he'd say, "Next time you do that, let me know what you take." That was all. He never had any problem with money.

When I moved out I was eighteen and Terry was a year and a half. The night before I left, Terrence and I had a discus-

sion. I told him, "I can't take your bullshit no more. You go
out, you stay out, you leave me here by myself with Terry,
and I really want you to be home with me sometimes." And,
too, I told him, "I can't take your mother neither. 'Don't do
this. Don't do that. You're not supposed to take care of a
child that way.' " She'd never let me be with Terry the way
I wanted. I'd be screamin' at her, "This is my child. I have to
learn!" In fact, you could say it like this—Terry's more or less
raised by them, by Terrence's mother and his stepfather, because they didn't give me that chance when I was there. So I
told him I'm leaving. And he started to cry, almost. "Leticia,
don't leave me. Don't ever leave." He was real upset. And,
too, I know he was very happy he had a baby, a little boy,
but still he was wanting to do his own thing—he didn't want
to grow up and face his responsibility. Yet he was working.
But I told him I needed to get out, get my own apartment,
so I didn't have to worry about what he was doing and where
he was going. Then, too, I have to say . . . and I feel that I
followed my mother in this . . . she used to see a lot of men,
and that's the same for me. Oh, yes, I seen a number of them.
I know, too, that's how my relationship broke up.

When I left Terrence, I got my own place. It was my grandmother Rena's. She had this apartment which she was renting out to someone else while she lived with my aunt. And I
begged her to let me have it. "I want this apartment so bad,"
I told her. "I'll take care of it. I'll be responsible." And I had
these fantasies, you know. I wanted so for Terry's father to
move in. I wanted so much to get married to him. But I was
living in a dream world.

My grandmother let me have the apartment, and I was
so pleased. My apartment was right across the street from my
mother's. And almost the first thing I did was call my friend
I had known for my whole life—she lived in my mother's
building. I said, "Dolores, I got my own place; we can hang
out more, be together." So then it seemed like all of a sudden

her mother kicked her out—and this girl was twenty-three at the time and I was only eighteen. And she came to me asking if she could move in. And I told her, "Come on, move in till you find a place, whatever." And it was innocent to me.

Before I knew it, after only a few months, her boyfriend started coming over, staying for days, and I didn't say anything, you know. And then he started giving me money, and the amount of money was very good. I don't think anybody would have turned down this money. He gave me a thousand dollars a week, and I was on public assistance, and I didn't tell them—I didn't say anything. I kept the thousand dollars, and at the time I had been paying the rent and buying food and everything. And I was already into drugs, just smoking marijuana, but I didn't have a bad habit like I did when I got in with that crowd.

Dolores's boyfriend found out that I was getting high, so he offered me this drug—it was a combination of marijuana mixed with crack—and when I tried it, it's like I just fell in love with it. I had to have more. It made me feel great. I was speedin' everywhere, constantly on the go. I had to find things to do, and I didn't sleep. I didn't eat, and at the time I was real heavy and I wanted to lose weight, and when I found this out, I got hooked. It took one week.

There was never a time that I didn't take it, so there weren't no symptoms like withdrawal or nothing. I started to taste it when it wasn't there. I got the urge to take it more and more, until I'd do anything to get it. So I started selling drugs for my friend's boyfriend. And it was out of *my* apartment. And I had a brand-new apartment, beautiful, brand-new building, and my rent was very reasonable—$195 a month—and my Con Ed wasn't so bad—$30 a month. And everything was so good at the beginning. I had plenty of food; my closets was full. And, too, Terrence used to smoke with me too. He knew about this. And what makes it so bad now, he denies everything. He makes it look like I'm the culprit, like he never touched anything.

But I had a bad habit, though, and it went on for nine months before I went to rehab. And I was doing things in between while I was taking the stuff. I was robbing them. I was taking money from the safe they had in the house. They had lots of crack, which this guy used to make out of cocaine and baking soda. Nowadays, people, they add more to it, and that really bugs the people out that takes it. They add $B_{12}$ and other things, and I've heard they add PCP. But when I took it, it was just baking soda and cocaine.

For a while they didn't know I could get into the safe. I used to use a steak knife. But then I would get high with my girlfriend, and when you're like that you start to jabber. You tell everything. So I told her I could get it for free, don't worry about it, I know how to get it. So she went and told on me, because there was jealousy. I could get it and it was there, and she couldn't. So she figured she'd tell, not knowing that was gonna stop everything—us getting high together. And she mentioned to me, she said So-and-so told her that I was taking this and taking that, and she mentioned it in front of her boyfriend. And I was kinda nervous because I didn't know what they were gonna do. They had guns in my house too— I was thinking they were gonna kill me, I was gonna be dead.

So finally I confessed. I told them yes, I did it, and if you had that amount of money and things in your house, and you were in it, you'd do the same thing. So her boyfriend was like, "No problem." He just took everything out—he took most all the drugs, he took the money, he took the guns. Then one night—by then they were getting ready to move out—there was a block party outside, and I had went with this other guy, and when I got back, I went into the block that they were selling drugs on, and I asked him if I could have a free crack, and he said he'd meet me at my apartment in two minutes, he gotta get the rest of his stuff. So I went up there and I waited, and they came—him and his part-ner—and they got the TVs out and some of the other stuff. I was sitting at the table, and his partner had taken fifteen hundred dollars from him, and some crack, and I didn't know it. But being that I had already robbed from him, I was accused. So he grabbed up a pipe and the TV antenna and beat me to death. I'll never forget that. I had both my arms broken and stitches. I called Terrence and he called my father and the cops came and they said I'd better move out of New York. But I said I didn't see no reason to move. And my father talked to the cops. And he took me to the hospital.

I never had the guy prosecuted. I guess I was too scared. But right after that happened, they did get arrested, and I didn't say anything. I didn't have to. They were on their way to New Jersey and they had drugs in the car, they had guns and whatnot, and they got caught. Then like six weeks after I got my casts off and my stitches had healed, I was back to doing the same thing—you'd think that I would have learned a lesson.

Truth is, I had caught myself trying to stop, but I didn't. I started hanging out with this other girl, Spanish girl, and that's when I started prostituting. And all this time now, my son was living with me.

That winter came by, and Terry was two and a half. I remember it was November, and my grandmother called me. She knew I was taking drugs—she had a feeling. She wasn't sure, but she came to me and asked me about it, and I told her yes, I was on drugs, and she told me, "Leticia, I think you should go into a rehab and let Terry go and stay at his aunt's house"—Terrence's sister. I didn't really want him to go, but I said OK. I knew I couldn't take care of him anymore. So I agreed to let him stay there but just for a weekend.

And I did go to a rehab, as an outpatient. I was there for about a week, but it wasn't good. After I'd leave, I'd go get high. Anyway, when Terry went over to his aunt's, I felt then I had the freedom to bring my clients into my home—parade all acts. Sometimes I would get depressed about what I was doing, but then I'd think about the money.

And I was gettin' good money! About five hundred dollars—not a client, maybe two clients together, two fifty apiece. I had a regular clientele I'd see all the time, regular customers, not standing on a street corner. I never did that—just to meet them, that's it. And I never had a pimp. I worked for myself. I had many guys say to me, "Let me watch out for you." That's what they say. But you end up having to give them money.

And I wanted my money. I like to have a lot of nice things. I'm very extravagant. I want everything I see that I like. I want it. And somehow I'm gonna get it. Like now I got my stereo, I got my color TV, my VHS. I'm not gonna say I'm money hungry, 'cause I'm not just gonna go and do anything to get money, but I like nice things.

I do say, too, that I feel I was never raised to work and go get the good things I want, 'cause my mother was buying everything from a thrift shop—our whole house, including my clothes—and I was embarrassed and I guess my mother, at the time, she couldn't afford it and she felt it was decent enough. I can accept that, but for my kids I want better, you know.

Even when I was tricking, there was this guy who tried to get me off drugs. He was on it too, but he could take it or leave it. And he tried to get me off seeing other guys. He was like, "You got me, why you need the other men?" " 'Cause it's money!" I told him. That's the way I was thinking. It's money.

# 6 ▪ *"Nobody talked about childbirth or sex"*

## Rena Wilson

*At sixty-three, Rena Wilson is an attractive woman with high cheek-bones, a full figure, and somewhat lighter skin than her daughter and granddaughter. The many times we met in her three-room apartment, she dressed conservatively, in navy blues or other dark colors. Her clothes were tailored, and everything about her person and her home was neat.*

*Mrs. Wilson's constrained and sober demeanor gives her an in-accessible quality. As she speaks, she looks into the distance. Very rarely did she show pleasure or delight, and when she did, it was only about two subjects: children and her father.*

*Rena Wilson puts a premium on self-control. She moves and speaks slowly and deliberately. She articulates each word about her past as if she had felt pain once but had hardened to it. Listening to her, I was struck, both by her keen personal sense of responsibility and by her feelings of disappointment and distrust. Her words and sentiments are those of a realist.*

When I gave birth to my first child, I didn't know whether she was going to be born from the front, back, or sideways.

I was eighteen years old and scared to death. This was 1942. Nobody talked about childbirth or sex. And if you were pregnant and not married, you weren't allowed to go out in the street. Flaunt yourself. And the older people never spoke of this. If they had an unmarried pregnant daughter, it was a very shameful thing. That's why I find it so hard to see these young women today practically joyous because they are this way. I don't understand it.

I was born in 1924. My given name was Mary Rena Wilson. In parochial school I was called Mary, and I hated it. Such a common name. And my middle name . . . my mother named me Rena after the daughter of a Jewish woman she worked for. That's the name she used at home, and that's the name that has stuck.

I lived in Washington, D.C., until I was about four years old. I can still remember taking a horse and buggy from Bushwood, Maryland, where my parents' families lived, to Washington. I have the most vivid memory of one of these rides because a little garden snake had gotten into the buggy and everyone was screaming and flailing. My mother says this didn't happen, but I do remember it.

We moved to New York City—Manhattan—but how we got here I can't say. We must have come by bus—my older sister, Eleanor, my parents, and me. What I remember about those first years is how often we moved. From 154th Street to 153rd to 152nd to 151st, then back to 152nd Street. But I could never understand *why* we moved so much until I got older—when I was an adult, in fact. An old school friend was telling me that during the Depression, most landlords where we lived offered three free months' rent to entice you to their building. I realized then that that was how we got our housing. I guess it was cheaper to pay the moving man. Anyway, the truth was that we had very little furniture. A table, a couch, and my sister and I shared a bed. Our apartment was neat but very plain.

Finally we moved to our last residence at 152nd Street, and that's where I grew up. I believe that building is still standing. It's boarded up now, but it's there. At one time, you know, it was such a nice section.

We were a very poor family. Often there was no food in the house. In fact, I think the only physical fight my sister and I ever had, we fought over food. There was some cocoa, and there was just enough bread to make an apple butter sandwich. But Eleanor wanted both, and I told her no. So we got to fighting. We tore up the bread and spilled the cocoa and neither of us had anything to eat. We got into a real fistfight over scraps of food.

It was the Depression when we moved to New York City, and I still recall how difficult it was for my father to find steady work. I used to watch him get up every morning to go out looking. He was a short-order cook. My father was the kind of man that when he had a job he would work every day. He didn't stay off from work unless he was sick. Unless it was absolutely necessary. He was conscientious, a hard worker. And I recall one of his bosses liked him very much. But things were so hard at that time that the boss had to give one of his relatives a job. So they threw Dad out. After that he would take on odd jobs. But they would end, and he'd have to go out looking again. He couldn't seem to find any real work.

I know his not working ate at him. Men in my father's era were taught to be the breadwinner. His parents had twelve children, and my father's father supported his family. And my grandmother never worked. She raised the children and helped around the farm. My father's father made good money. He used to dig wells, grow tobacco, and sell some of his crops. He owned his own land. His parents were of American Indian descent, and I recall they had quite a few acres when they died. There were about nine or ten children left, and the property had to be divided between them. But it was easier to support a family when you had land. When you grew your own food and had housing.

My father's unemployment was terribly hard on him. And I think what happened at that time was that a lot of men couldn't find work, so they would go downtown and congregate. And for something better to do, maybe, they'd stop and have a drink, and one drink led to another. After a while my father became so depressed he started drinking heavily. He became an alcoholic.

My father started staying away from home more and more, and I remember that my mother and sister and I would go out looking for him, asking people if they had seen him. Sometimes they'd tell us he was in the hospital. And we would find him there, bruised and torn up.

My father left for good when I was thirteen. When I entered high school, he just disappeared. We couldn't find him anywhere. I remember we went looking for him, days and weeks. It's hard to recall just how long it was. But I would say it was about six months to a year before we actually knew where he was. One of his relatives in Maryland finally told us his sister had taken him back to his mother.

"They took him away from his own home," my mother used to tell us. She was very upset about it and never forgave him or them. But my being young, all I knew was that my father was gone. I used to go try to visit him at my grandmother's when I found out where he was. But sometimes I would see him there and sometimes I wouldn't. I was devastated when he left.

I loved my father very dearly. I still do. He's eighty-eight years old and senile. He lives in Queens now, and I visit him quite often. His sister still takes care of him.

I always thought my father was a good father. He was a very quiet man, what I knew of him, a person who would sit down and listen to you but didn't talk too much himself. Very seldom did he raise his voice, unless something terrible went wrong. And he didn't believe in beating you and arguing, which my mother believed in. Beating you within an inch of your life! When my father used to get dressed up, I felt so proud walking down the street with him. He was tall, six feet, with black wavy hair. He was very handsome.

My father was a musician. He played the violin. In fact, my mother told me that when they lived in Maryland, he played with this orchestra, the John B. Young Orchestra. And in New York he used to fiddle and another friend played the banjo. Every so often they would have these little get-togethers at home. It was a very nice thing.

My father taught my sister and I how to dance. He taught us how to waltz, to do the two-step. He took us to our first dance. And often he took us to church and to the church dances. And he danced with us, you know. And a few times he took us to the Roxy Theater. My father took us most places that we went. Almost all of our socializing was done through him. I remember this because most fathers were off someplace, but before he got real bad, my father was usually home. Certainly on Sunday.

My mother, now, she was another story. She was the disciplinarian in the family. My relationship to her has always been more complicated. I'm still not sure what I think about her. What she thinks of me.

As a child, I always thought she was real strict. Too strict. She was always beating me for something. Like when I went to parochial school, a lot of times I would have to go to the bathroom other than when we went with the monitor. But the sister wouldn't let me go. A couple of times I remember I just pulled down my pants in the class and peed on the floor. I got a beating from my mother for that! But I felt justified. I didn't want to wet on my clothes, soil them, because in those days we wore those union suits with three buttons across and panties, plus heavy stockings, and I would have been a mess.

And her strictness showed in this too: she forbade us to fight with anybody. And I was always getting into trouble. I was a tomboy. I had a nasty temper, and I was much more feisty and rambunctious than my sister. Eleanor was two years older than I was, but she never really fought with anyone. Just one time, when a boy hit me in my glasses, she did go into the street to get him.

But the kids on our block always knew that I would fight and especially that my mother didn't want me to. They knew I was going to hit back. They would bully me, push me. They'd get all up in my face and start shoving me. Then soon as I got started, they'd run upstairs and tell my mother, and she'd whip me with a belt. I'd tell her, "Nobody is going to hit me, or I'm going to hit them back!" But she'd just holler, "No fighting!" So whenever I got to battling, I made up my mind I was going to get a licking and that was it. It made me very resentful, though. I felt I was always a target.

But I know, too, that my mother had a lot of responsibilities. And I used to remind myself of that to reconcile myself to her actions. She supported our family when my father couldn't find work. And after he left. She did domestic work, and at one point she worked in a dressmaking factory. She brought home our food. And besides, in that particular era many mothers were strict. I think a person could identify with getting a whipping. Your friend across the hall got one too.

Of course, I did have friends who didn't get beatings. And I noticed that. Some of them had parents who were much friendlier to their children. They were able to sit down and talk to each other. In our house it was "Shut up! Don't ask questions." And I was a curious child, so it was a difficult situation. Really very frustrating.

———

But besides being strict, my mother was and still is a big card-player, so she didn't have much time with us. In the evening after work, sometimes she wouldn't get home until we were in bed. We wouldn't see her till way late. And the times we would see her was if we left the dishes or something out. She would come and get us out of our bed and make us do them.

I had a lot of feelings about my mother being out. Playing cards. I remember in high school sitting there, thinking about my parents separating. Sometimes I used to wonder maybe the combination of my father not having a job and not having a wife to stay home with—that all this was the reason he left.

When I started Wadleigh High School, I almost had a nervous breakdown thinking about my father. Sometimes I stayed out of school completely. He was so much on my mind. His cousin kept telling us he was in and out of hospitals down South, and I would be worrying, Is he going to live or die?

I remember I had a hard time concentrating in school when I did go. Also because my subjects were much harder than they were in parochial school. They did not come easy to me. Then, too, often I was hungry. I remember I would get these terrific headaches. My mother would always give us something to eat for breakfast, but if there wasn't any money that day, I didn't get lunch. By the time the afternoon classes came around, I remember feeling tired and weak. It was too long to go without food.

And, too, when I first started public school, I felt scared to death. I was thrown in with all these girls that acted differently from what I had been used to. The Jewish girls just stayed to themselves. The blacks, some were good and some bad. And then there were lesbians. In my other school, everybody knew each other. It was smaller and friendlier. I really felt very overwhelmed when I changed.

I think, though, that one of the things that made me most upset, and this was all through my growing up, was the ways my mother favored my sister. It made me mad. She wasn't as strict with her as she was with me. If my sister had homework to do, then I had to do the dishes and the housework. Why was I the one who always had to run to the store?

My mother doted on the fact that my sister was the smarter of the two of us. When there was money to be had, she used it on my sister first. And I resented it. In fact, I mentioned it to my mother on any number of occasions, but she'd just say, "Well, after all, your sister is going to a very good high school and she is an A-plus student." [Eleanor went to Hunter High School, a school for which you needed a high IQ and high scores on an entrance examination.] I'd call my mother trying to explain it away. But her explanation was never good enough for me. I resented having to wear one dress for a whole term, where my sister had clothes to choose from.

The thing was, my sister was smarter. I don't take that away from her. She was the type of person that if she didn't get one hundred on a test, she'd cry. Subjects came much easier to her. My resentment came because I felt that even if I wasn't as smart, I should have had some recognition for trying. I did my homework. I never failed a class. But my mother didn't show me the same interest and affection she did my sister. "Am I adopted?" I'd always ask her that. And she'd just yell, "No! Where do you get this foolishness from?" But I was always a child who would speak my mind, whether you broke my jaw!

# 7 ▪ *"I remember hiding under the biggest coat"*

---

# Rena Wilson

Darren Randall looked a lot like my father. He was tall and even more handsome and a very good dancer. I started seeing him a year and a half after my father left. We were both the same age, about fifteen. Darren was a very motivated and ambitious young man. He talked about going to college, and he was already earning his own money, working in a candy store after school. We'd meet every afternoon when we got off our jobs. I was working part-time in a doctor's office.

But Darren and I weren't supposed to date. My mother was very strict about this. And I recall, too, my father telling me when I was much younger not to get serious about any boy until I was sixteen or seventeen. In fact, I believe that's when he and my mother got married. But Darren and I knew each other from our parochial school. We both belonged to an alumni association, and they used to give dances on Friday and Saturday nights. So we'd meet each other there too. And he did come to my house.

We spent a great deal of time together. Darren's parents

were also separated, and I remember sitting on the stoops of our buildings, talking about how much we missed our fathers, wishing they were back again. His father had left a few years earlier, and his mother was in show business. She was a dancer, and she was never around. Both of us were lonely, and I think more than anything that's what brought us together. We were very close.

On several occasions, I remember, Darren pressed me for sex. But most of what Darren and I did together was talk. We kissed too, and when we went to the movies, he'd put his arm around me. But there was none of this petting and mauling like there is today.

Then about a year and a half after I met Darren, he started pressing me for sex. He'd put me to the test. "We can't go together anymore," he'd say. "All the other Catholic girls are doing this and that." But I didn't believe him. And I knew what my mother had told me. In those days, if you got pregnant you were a real outcast.

So I'd say no, but then he'd always threaten to break off the relationship. He'd stay away for two or three days at a time, and in those days neither of us had telephones, so we'd have no contact. Then he would come back and apologize. "It will never happen again," he'd promise. But we broke up several times over this sex issue, because I continued to say, "No. We will get married, then sex will come."

In our senior year, though, I do recall that we secretly began talking of getting married. Having our own apartment. In those days, when you went out with a fellow for a year or two, in our circles of friends, it was taken for granted that eventually you would marry. Most of our classmates got married shortly after they graduated high school. Around eighteen or nineteen, even seventeen. Some went to college. And it was also wartime. A lot of the young men were going into service. So getting married was very important if you wanted to keep your fellow.

––––––––

Finally I did submit to Darren. It may have been a weaker moment for me—not a passionate moment, because I remember no thoughts of wanting sex. I had not entered into sex with anyone. Darren, in fact, was the only beau I had in high school. No, it wasn't passion. It was one of those things where he said, "I'll stick by you through thick and thin, and I'll see to it that nothing happens." I suppose I wanted to believe him. I wanted to feel that human closeness.

And in some ways, too, I was very naive about sex. No one had ever really sat down with me and explained the details of sex. All my mother used to say was, when you have your period, stay away from boys. So that's what I did. I thought she meant *that's* when you could get pregnant. My mother did have a medical book, and so did the office I worked in. And I used to read through them. But in a way they weren't about sex. They were about anatomy. They talked about a sperm and an egg. But what was a sperm and an egg? You know what I mean? I didn't think it had anything to do with me, with my body.

What I remember about having intercourse was that Darren had to tell me how to do it. And I remember the terrible pain, the fright, and saying to myself, "If this is sex, I don't care for it."

At that time in my life, I was very unrealistic. I remember putting off any action about telling my mother until the last possible moment. And I was petrified about her reaction. I remember I got sick a couple of times, but fortunately she wasn't around much. But I did tell the doctor I worked for, in order to ascertain the truth. He examined me and said, "Yes, you are pregnant."

I just recall being so frantic. I went to tell Darren then, but he said, "Don't worry. We're going to get married and live together." So I recall that I felt more comfortable with it.

But I still had to tell my mother. I knew I couldn't tell her outright, so I devised a letter and left it on her dresser. She came home very late that night and stormed into my room. "What do you mean, you're pregnant!" she yelled. "You were taught better. That baby can't come into this house!" It was a real scene.

I explained to her that Darren and I were going to get married. So her first step was to see Darren's mother. But as soon as his mother found out about the pregnancy, she made plans to spirit Darren away. Right after, she sent him to live with an aunt in Long Island. I remember thinking for many months that he would come forth. Keep his promise. But he never did. I never saw him after that—not for twenty years, when my daughter Enid was getting married and asked to meet her father. He sent a couple of hundred dollars for the wedding and came by to see me several times. He apologized, but what did that matter then? Anything I had felt for him I had wiped out of my mind. I'm the type of person, if you don't love me, I won't have anything to do with you. I don't like to live a lie.

When my mother realized Darren wasn't going to marry me, she informed me I would have to give the child up for adoption. But that was never my decision! I was going to keep my child. I wasn't just going to throw her away. So my mother let me know that I couldn't live at home when I started showing and that she wouldn't have my baby in her house.

But of course, that wasn't unusual for those times. Often when a young lady got pregnant, she'd be sent to a home for unwed mothers. If she was allowed to stay at home after her child was born, her parents made up some excuse about the baby when it came. "Oh, this is a relative's child," they'd say, or, "We're just taking in this baby for a while."

I graduated high school two months pregnant. And as it turned out, my mother did allow me to live at home until the baby came. I still remember, when I started showing, except for one or two people, no one was allowed to visit me. And when

I went to my clinic visits, I remember hiding under the biggest coat I could find. In fact, I went to the clinic only twice when I was showing, because my mother was afraid someone would see me. If it wasn't for the health nurse who used to visit us every month or so to bring us vitamins—check on our food and how we were getting along—I wouldn't have been allowed to go to the clinic at all.

Before I started showing, though, I went to work. I was determined to get a job right after I graduated. To save money for my child and me. I remember my friend and I went through all the want ads, and I found a job working in a factory, ironing appliqués on dresses. It was horrible. I had to scorch off the thick mesh on the back of the designs with a knife, then steam the appliqués onto the cloth. It was the end of June and very hot. But the worst part was the Jewish man who owned the factory. He used a lot of profanity. "What do I have to do?" he'd yell. "Stick a pin in your ass to make you work faster?" After two months I couldn't stand it any longer, and I quit. I went to work in another factory, this time counting buttons.

I started showing a few months later, though, and my mother forbid me to leave the house. So for the next four months I was basically isolated. I was in hiding. I was scared. I kept wondering how this baby was going to be born. The two clinic visits weren't helpful. In those days, they didn't describe the birth procedures, or if they did, I didn't attend those classes. All I remember them saying was, "Come into the hospital when you start feeling sharp pains." So that's what I kept waiting for, but they never came. In fact, I remember one night I just kept feeling like I had to go to the bathroom. I kept getting in and out of bed, until my mother started saying, "What's wrong with you? Is the baby coming?" But I just said no, because I didn't feel any sharp pains.

Finally my mother did decide to take me to the hospital.

And I was already three weeks overdue. When I got there I remember hearing all these women screaming and yelling, and I thought, Oh, no, the worst is yet to come. But it never did. Aside from some pains in my back, I never even went into labor. My waters broke, and my baby was born an hour later.

I hadn't picked out a name. So my mother suggested Enid, after another daughter of a Jewish woman she had worked for. Since my mother and I had this understanding that I couldn't come home with the baby, the health nurse suggested we go to Misericordia, a home for unwed mothers.

It was a very nice place, I remember. The nuns took good care of us, and they had very pleasant dormitory facilities for the mothers and babies. I lived there with Enid for six months. But during that time you were supposed to come to some decision about your baby. Whether you were going to give it up for adoption or go home with it. Since I couldn't bring her home, I had to put Enid into the foundling home. She stayed there for another six months. I visited her almost every evening after I finished work at Chock Full o'Nuts.

All the time she was there, though, I kept thinking about how I was going to get her out. I knew my only real opportunity would be to get married. So that's what I did. I married Lewis Cadden, a virtual stranger. I didn't know much about Lewis except that he had a job. A friend of mine had introduced us, and we went out on a couple of dates. I told him I had a child, and he and I would go to visit Enid together.

Lewis told me a number of lies, like he was an orphan and that he didn't have any brothers or sisters. He told me he had been fending for himself for years. I was never sure why he made up these stories—as it turned out, he had a mother and a father. Maybe he wanted me to feel sorry for him, to stick with him. Anyway, when he proposed marriage I jumped at the chance. The day after we married, we picked up Enid and brought her home to my mother's house. The marriage lasted a year.

# 8 ▪ *"God didn't say people should have children and not be married"*

## Louise Eaton

The first time Louise Eaton greeted me at her red-brick house in Queens, she was carefully unrolling her wispy gray hair from pin curlers. "Don't want it to fly away," she said, laughing. At eighty-three, Mrs. Eaton, as she likes to be called, is a woman who has a "hot spot" for men. She didn't hesitate to tell me that her "gentleman caller" was coming by later that afternoon.

Sexy and flirtatious, Mrs. Eaton chuckles over her naughtiness, "my little pleasures of life." Her humor and her ready gleefulness are contagious. It's impossible to be with her for more than a minute or two without joining her in her sexual banter. "Your husband taking good care of you?" she asked, her eyebrows popping.

Louise Eaton is indeed a character. The glint in her brown eyes is matched only by her seductive laugh and her charming Southern drawl. But she can be as sober as she is funny. Her open face closes down abruptly when she talks of the poor, or the physical hardship of others. And she is quick to separate her own problems from the trials of those "more unfortunate." Indeed, it was only on second glance that I noticed her difficulty in walking. Admitting to a badly ulcerated leg, she would have preferred to deny her infirmity.

*As we ate our first lunch together, one that she had taken great pains to make, Mrs. Eaton pointed out the gifts and the religious icons her family and her many friends have given her over the years. In the end, Louise Eaton is as religious as she is sexy, as serious as she is funny.*

Darlin', I've been a Catholic all my life. That's why I know how to live. I know what God tells me from the Bible. He has blessed me. Not everyone knows this man like I do. And sometimes I have to say I'm bad, real bad, 'cause I fuss with Him when He doesn't give me what I ask for. And I ask Him for kids. That's how I got my money, you know. Oh, yes. I took in kids. Every time I pray to God, I pray for children.

Once I had ten children in this house. Mothers used to leave their children with me, and I cared for them the same way I did my own. You have to care for children right, 'cause they can't take care of themself. That's why I love them.

And I believed in rules. You have to. Without rules, children have nothing. Look at these mothers today. They don't know how to bring up their children. You think I would walk around with those little short things above my knees? Never! And I'd never wear pants. God didn't tell me to wear no pants. You've got to respect yourself. And your children. Today's kids *rule* their mothers. They don't have a child's life.

I brought up my own children strict. They went to Catholic schools, so they didn't act up or they would get my strap. My children are good. Never had trouble with them. No jail. No hospital. Nothin'. And Eleanor, my older child, is a college graduate. I'm blessed. If you believe in God, you get diamonds, rubies, and pearls. God has always said to me, "Louise, you behave yourself and I'll take care of you." So that's the way I live, because I don't want His punishment.

And my life has never been hard. I won't hear of that! I'm a Maryland girl, you know. St. Mary's County, 'bout sixty-five miles out of Washington, D.C. I'm a country girl. Just simple.

That's the way I am. And I'll tell you there was nothin' like country life. When I was a child, if I didn't have somethin' to eat on my table—and we always did have meat, because we had hogs, chickens, and cows—but if I didn't have somethin' to eat, I would take my little basket to a neighbor's house and he would give me apples, potatoes, greens. He'd give me cabbage. You don't find that today. All those poor people lying in the streets. I saw a lady with six children outside on the pavement. How can children grow up like this? You know, God put aplenty in this world for all of us, and when you elect a President, you want more. You want someone to talk straight. You want him to *care* for the poor. You want him to provide jobs and housing. People should learn a trade, something else besides books. Look at Russia—those boys are seven years old and are training. That's what we should have in our schools—one hour a day. People want to feel good about themselves, about what they can do. People can't work for $3.50 an hour anymore. Maybe you can get something to eat, but how could you pay these rents today?

Myself, I had twelve brothers and sisters. My father had a farm. We lived in a small wooden country house. Just a few rooms. The children slept in a bed or on the floor. I can't tell you if I was clean or dirty as a very young child. How exactly I was brought up. Those times are misty. But I do remember I went to church and I made my first Communion. And I remember the day my mother passed.

I was three years old, but it's still with me. I was sittin' on the front porch, and she came home from work. It was about four or five in the late afternoon, and she came onto the porch. Sat herself on a small stool or a little box. I remember her clothes was loose, 'cause it was a very hot day and my mother was stout. She asked one of the children to bring her the baby. But before she could nurse him, she fell over dead. They ran to tell my grandmother down the road. But she couldn't take the news. They had a double funeral. I remember my mother's brother arriving by phaeton, late for the funeral, and so many people comin' to our house. A woman walked over to me. She kneeled me down and we said our prayers.

I used to work alongside my father in the fields. And I had a good time doin' it. Used to cut tobacco, shuck corn. And I went to school, but I had my chores to do. I'd get up real early, five in the mornin'. And I had chores in the evenin' after my lessons. But I only made the eighth grade, 'cause I couldn't go no further than that at the time.

I recall we had an arbor, and I would think about that fruit, the grapes and all that stuff. And my father was an oysterer in the winter. He'd go in the river and catch those oysters with his great tongs and sell them. And he taught me how to shuck them. You always shuck oysters from the back. But after my mother died . . . you know how men are, they let things go down—till my father didn't do practically anythin'.

But I used to have a lot of fun with him. Sometimes we'd be staying up to three or four in the morning singing songs. And my father passed at eighty-nine, and even after I'd come back to visit, I'd ask him to sing those old songs, and he'd say, "I don't know if I know them still, girl." But he did. Oh, we used to have so much fun. We were very close, you know.

After a time, most all the children left the farm. I left rather early too. About thirteen or fourteen. I went to live with a sister in another part of St. Mary's County for a year or so, and then after that I moved to another sister in Washington, D.C. I had kids there. I used to take in children. Take them to the park, feed them, care for them. So that was my life. I worked eight hours a day. It was hard, but that wasn't my question. My question was, Did God bring me these children? Did He give me this way of earnin' my money?

My sister lived with her husband and six children, so

things were kinda poor. I had to work in the marsh to make extra money. I used to go there and pick two or three sacks of watercress at a time. Bendin' and bendin', but the Lord was with me. I knew He was takin' care. And I went chestnut and walnut huntin' and picked persimmons on Sunday. And I remember pickin' three or four buckets of blackberries to sell to the white people for twenty-five cents a bucket. I'm still so mad when I think that my sister didn't tell me different. A big water bucket of berries for twenty-five cents! They just robbed you.

At the end of that year, though, I got me a real fine situation. A woman asked me if I would move into her home and care for her baby. Oh, I was so excited! They had such a beautiful home: a cook, a pool table, and I had a room to myself and a bath. The first privacy I had in my life. And I loved it. But the woman also had a teenage boy. And one night, after a few months, he snuck into my room. Came right into my bed! He started pullin' the covers one way while I was pullin' them the other. I was petrified and so dumb, so naive. All I could think of telling him was to come back the next night, and by then I was gone. I was so scared, I never even told the woman what happened.

So I moved back to my sister's again. It always seemed that I was moving from one place to another. But I knew she was too poor to take me. I started takin' care of kids again to help, and I wouldn't say it was hard, you know, but sometimes it was difficult. She had a small place, and there was just too many of us to feed. I was about fifteen or so at the time, and that's when I met William.

William Chambers was a short-order cook. He had a real job and was supportin' hisself. His family was from St. Mary's County, and I did know them a bit. He was six years older than me, and he was a *fine* dancer. In fact, we met at a dance hall, where my friends and I would go from time to time.

And I remember he approached me, and when we started dancin', he dared put his hand on my behind! Well, I almost left him right there on the floor. A woman has to be a woman! But I knew God sent me a nice man.

We courted for a short time, maybe a year or less. But those times were so different. You can't imagine how stupid we were about sex. Especially the girls. Not that we weren't interested in young men. We were just scared. And I can still recall William sayin', "What kind of woman are you that I couldn't put my hand back there?" But that's just how I was. Of course, some people did have their goings-on, but people just didn't act the way they do today. People had a privacy to them. Girls had a kind of shyness.

William and I went to Baltimore to get married. I was sixteen, and a year later, in 1922, Eleanor was born. I knew quite a lot of girls who got married young and had children. It wasn't a bad thing, nothin' unusual. Just hard. And if you were a poor person, there wasn't the kind of help you have today. No welfare, of course. We had to do things on our own.

But I can tell you, we wouldn't of *thought* of havin' a child without bein' married, like so many of these girls are today. All this dope and sex. You can smell marijuana over the streets. On the buses! God didn't say people should have children and not be married. Of course, He also said if you give a life you can't take it. But these days it's the check. I can understand one mistake. Ever'body can make one. But not two. Bringin' children into the world and you can't care for them. It's a sin in the eyes of the Lord. In my times, if a girl got pregnant and she didn't have a husband, she found one! Or if she remained single, she went into a home. Her pregnancy was a secret thing. Girls laced theirself up tight as they could!

For a few years, William and I had a real good marriage. I didn't love him at first, but I grew to. He gave me my family. We'd go to the dance halls with our friends, and for twenty-five cents you could stay and have a real nice time. We lived in a little place in Washington, just a couple of rooms. It wasn't fancy. But it was home, and we had our privacy.

At the time, William worked and I took care of Eleanor. I was so close to her! I used to hold her all the time, till a lady at the doctor's office told me, "Put that child down. Let her get some dirt on her." Havin' a mother is a beautiful thing. In my own life I had the Blessed Mother.

By the time Rena came, I had learned a little more. She was born two years after Eleanor. But these times were beautiful to me. I was growing up with my children, and I loved it. And this time they was my own!

A while after Rena was born, though, it just started seemin' that William wasn't makin' enough money. So I had to go to work. And I know, too, that God wanted me to stay home with my children. But I couldn't carry out His wishes.

I did domestic work, just the same as my mother. And we got people to care for the children. And sometimes my sister would watch them. But it just seemed that no matter how hard we tried, though, we couldn't seem to make ends meet. We were always quarreling about money. And I can remember bein' down on my knees scrubbin' floors, wonderin' if I would ever have a house of my own, whether I could care for my children myself. It seemed that there were times that we all but gave up. But the Lord was takin' care of us in His way. I thanked God every day. And I told Him one thing—if I have a lot or a little, whatever I have, I'm gonna live with it.

William and I talked over our problems, and we decided the only way was for him to go to New York and look for work there. So that's what he did. His sister was up there, and he moved in with her while he looked for a job. And I recall it took several months for him to find one before he sent for us. But then he did.

I was real excited about movin' to New York! As a young girl I always thought New York was right behind the back of those hills. I was the only one in my family who ever moved north.

And, too, I was glad in some ways to be leavin' Washington. At that time it wasn't a very nice place to us, you know. It didn't treat colored people too well. I remember when I was pregnant with Eleanor going into a diner for a glass of water. It was the summertime and real hot. When I asked the man for some, he said to me, "Did you bring your own cup?" I didn't get a drop.

And a time when William and I went into a restaurant and the man showed us to the back but I wanted to sit in the front. I started to protest, you know, and William tugged on my arm and whispered for me to stop. He told me he didn't want to go to jail. Those things never bothered me, though. I called upon the dignity of my own person. God says we're a nation of people. He didn't say blacks or whites or yellows.

We moved to Harlem in the Great Depression. William got one job and then he'd lose it and go get another one, and then he would lose that too. And we'd be movin' from one place to another, till I couldn't stand the movin' anymore. Every time we'd turn around we'd be in a new place. We couldn't pay the rent.

And, too, we started fightin' again. And I knew William was losin' respect for hisself, not being able to support his family, like his father. But you know, his father was a well digger, and he had land. And when you have land, you have food and a roof over your head.

Myself, I went to work in a dress factory. They trained us to cut sleeves or sometimes backs. We never got to make a whole garment ourselves. And the money wasn't good, but it did bring in food. I hated it, but I stuck with it for six years. I was afraid to look for somethin' else for fear we'd all go hungry. I take my hat off to all women. We know how to survive.

But things was gettin' worse. William was taking any job that he could find, and he would contribute some of the money he was makin'. But then he was drinkin' too, stayin' out, and the girls and me, we would have to go out and bring him back. Then after a while he'd go again, and he'd be gettin' beat up. It was a terrible thing, and everyone was real upset. We loved him dearly.

When he left the last time, he went back to Maryland, to his parents. His sister came and got him and just took him away. We didn't even know his whereabouts. All I remember is going to church, puttin' a dime in, and prayin' to the Blessed Mother for him to come home. But he never did. You know, though, it wasn't like today. I mean you've gotta take some things. The way that people are today, they don't take anything. They just get up and leave. William wasn't a bad man. He was a good person. But he had his problems. And sometimes if you're weak, you just fall by the wayside. The devil is so strong . . . so strong.

# 9 ▪ *"I felt that loss"*

## *Leticia Johnson*

The drugs, the prostituting, gettin' beat up—all this happened to me in nine months, from May 1985 to February 1986. Sometimes I say to myself, I was so young—how could all that happen?

Then by February my habit had got so bad I went into another rehab. I stayed there for that month. Not the two years you're supposed to. But I feel you don't necessarily have to stay in for the length of time they tell you, if in your heart and your mind you know you're not gonna take it no more.

When I came out I went to the Y, the same place I was when Terry was first born. I went to live with my father's mother, Doreen, for a few months, 'cause I didn't have nowhere to go. When my counselor at the Y found out I had left rehab, she referred me to a place for drug counseling. They sent me to a residence called Westin House. I stayed there for April. Then I moved into Terrence's sister's house for one month. Then back to my mother's. In July I found out I was pregnant. About thirteen weeks. I remember it was July, just before Terry turned three years old.

---

I tried to stay at my mother's house, but it was too difficult. One night when I was getting up to go to the bathroom and I had on my robe and my nightgown, my stepfather was coming out of his room at the same time. All he had on was a coat. Nothing underneath, 'cause he let the coat fall open. I closed my eyes and turned back around and went in my room. I couldn't sleep that night out of fear. I was helpless. I was pregnant. What could I possibly do? So I got up the next morning real early and called my grandmother Rena. I told her I wanted to leave. She came and got me, and it was decided that I would move out to my great-grandmother Louise's house in Queens until the middle of February. After that I moved back to my mother's just for a couple of weeks, until Hazela was born. Then back again to Queens. I was moving all over the United States, right here in New York City.

Hazela was born in March '87, and it was like taking care of my child for the first time. I always felt Terry was more or less raised by Terrence's mother and his stepfather. That he belonged to them. That they didn't give me that chance when I was there.

Then, too, at the time I got pregnant, Terry wasn't with me. He was still with them. I didn't feel close with him 'cause they had cared for him for the months I was on crack. I felt that loss. I felt like I didn't have nobody. Like my son would never be with me again in my life. So I said, I'm gonna get pregnant again.

And the thing is, at the time I just wasn't thinking. I wanted a child so bad that I stopped taking my birth control. And Terrence and me, we had always planned, no matter what we went through, we was gonna have kids together. We weren't gonna have kids by nobody else. Even if we weren't together in a relationship. So I messed with Terrence, and we weren't even together. He was seeing another girl, and I was with this guy Gavin, who was twenty-seven years old.

But I told Terrence, "I want another baby." And he was like, "No, Leticia, I'm not ready. I can't take care of another one." So I lied to him that I was using the pill. And I got pregnant. And when he found out, he was real upset. He started yellin', "That's not my child!" And he said he wanted to pay for an abortion. But I told him no.

But then, I have to say, it's not absolutely certain that it is Terrence's child. Like I mentioned, I met this other guy, Gavin. And it was a strange night.

I was going out with Terrence that evening, and I was waiting for Terrence to pick me up at Westin House. I was dressed and ready. But before he came, I went to the store. I was speaking to a guy there, and Gavin was standing to the side. He came up to me and asked me what my name was. He said he'd seen me all the time 'cause he lived across the street from Westin House. And we used to see him every morning going to work. The girls used to call him out the window. I just had peeked at him, but I never thought I would meet him and then start going out with him.

When I was talking to Gavin, Terrence pulled up, with his spotlight from the car beaming on me, and I was like, "Oh, God, he caught me." But I was only talking to Gavin. So I got in the car with Terrence and he said, "What you doin' talkin' to that guy? That's your boyfriend now?" So I said, "No, I met him not too long before you came." So after that, in the next couple of days, Gavin and I started seeing each other. Our relationship only lasted like a week or two. And I was seeing Terrence a little then too.

Funny thing is, this weekend when Terrence saw Hazela, really got a good look at her for the first time, he said, "You know, Leticia, it's a possibility that that is my daughter." And I said,

"Possibility! It *is* your child!" 'Cause I had showed him a baby picture of Terry and one of Hazela, and he couldn't tell them apart even though they don't look nothing alike. She has light-colored eyes and skin and Terry doesn't, and nobody in Terrence's family does. But the way I feel is she's here now. And maybe she is his child, and whether he was ready or not, she arrived.

# PART II

*Coping:*
## Month to Month

*Each of the following dates, from
July 1987 through March 1988,
reflects one of my meetings with
Leticia over this nine-month
period.*

# 10 ■ *"If you hurt me, you're gonna feel it"*

## Leticia Johnson

**JULY 10, 1987** I'm living in Queens with my great-grand-mother Louise and Hazela and Terry. Hazela is four months old, and Terry's fourth birthday is coming in two weeks. The court gave me temporary custody of him 'cause I haven't been on drugs for a year and a half.

I love it out here. The outdoors. The trees. The quiet. Some-times I just lay down on the grass under the stars. I feel more secure. Like I told my nana, "It's so open. I don't feel like I'm trapped. Like I'm closed up." When I go into Manhattan, everybody's pushing and shoving. You could just be walking down the street and feel a hand.

I know that staying out here is better for me than going back to Manhattan. But then again, I just don't know. My privacy is one thing that's important to me. Trying to be re-sponsible to myself and my kids. I'm twenty years old, and sometimes, you know, it seems like I should be out there doing it on my own. I have depended on my grandmother, especially, for so long. But then, I'll tell you the truth, I don't know how I got this far. A lot of times I was close to death.

Sometimes I kinda wonder, though, am I ready to have an apartment, being that I messed up the first time? And the area that I'd be moving into is close to where I used to always come up to get crack. But I could get it here, too, if I wanted. There's temptation around! But regardless of where I move, that's not what I want, so I'm not going to do it again.

Anyway, I feel my life's more together now. I'm more settled in my ways. I don't go out and just meet any people. I'm so afraid I might get myself with the wrong person. At first they could be nice—people put on a front and pretend to be nice—and after a while they just try to hurt you. I'm leery of who I deal with. Who I talk to. I just don't want to be in no more bad situations. The next time that I get into one, I may not be able to get out.

And I'm going to the Y again. There's about thirteen or fourteen of us young mothers who come regularly. Most of us except me and two other girls have one child. We have two.

I started coming here when I was living with Terrence. One of the girls where my mother lives told me about it. So I've been here like three and a half years, off and on. I still didn't graduate yet. And I'm the oldest one here, so I'm getting impatient. But hopefully, I'll get my diploma in six months. January 1988—oh, yes!

I like the place a lot. The other day we had our end-of-the-year celebration, and I got two awards. One for leadership. The other for debating. In our parenting classes, we debate. We bring up issues like child neglect, sleeping habits, beating your child. Some girls actually think you should beat your child. But I don't, personally. Sometimes I may smack Terry if I tell him like three times don't do a certain thing and he continues to constantly do it. Then I hit his hand or his leg. But I don't beat him with a belt or anything, like my mother beat me. With a leather strap and ironing cords. Ugh. Just to think of that again!

I take classes here in the mornings. The basics. Math, reading, social studies, English, computers. All those subjects, 'cause I'm gonna get my GED [General Equivalency Diploma]. Then in the afternoons different people come speak to us. A lawyer from family court. A nurse who talks about contraception. Then on Wednesdays we have vocational, careers, schools, and colleges. There's a staff person who helps a lot of girls get jobs if they want to work. Or she helps them get into a college. Every Thursday the child-care person tells us how our kids are doing. And there's a day-care program just down the hall from our classroom, so I bring Hazela here with me and I can visit her when I want to.

They see me as a leader here 'cause I've been here so long. And 'cause I speak up. Like they ask me to be on panels, to talk about teenage pregnancy, to go to other schools, and to talk to politicians, you know. The girls turn to me with questions or to be their spokesperson, 'cause I'm not shy. I say what's on my mind.

Only thing is, like I say, I'm getting frustrated to finish, to be on my own. I'm thinking like I might be a cosmetologist. I love fixing people's hair. I could train and work at the same time. Or I think about being an artist, 'cause I've won awards in school for my drawings. Then, too, the woman who used to be the head of this program promised me a job at the Department of Health when I get my diploma. And that would be perfect!

The thing now that's bothering me, though, is getting custody of Terry. When I took him over to his aunt Sylvia's house that time I was on drugs, they petitioned for custody. But his aunt didn't get it. She got temporary custody. And then when I filed to get him back after my circumstances changed and I wasn't on drugs, they wouldn't give him back. So I filed for custody. Then right after that, Terrence filed too, 'cause his sister told him to. But the judge gave me temporary custody starting in May, until this court thing now in July.

When I think about this custody business, it makes me sick. At the time I was on crack, Terrence told me, "Your grandmother's gonna take your son, and you're never gonna see him." And all along it was him and his mother and Sylvia who was thinking of things to do to me. And this is one of the things that Terrence and me discussed when I had Terry. I told him, "Terrence, I don't feel I would ever take you to court under any circumstances 'cause you are taking care of Terry. You are supporting him. I have no problems with that." He recognized that he was the father, so what reason would I have to take him to court for? And me and him discussed this, and no one was around when we did. So when he took me to court, I asked him, "Remember when we discussed this? It was a bond between me and you." This hurts me now. He's trying to take my child away.

So now I am taking *him* to court. And I see he is upset. But I think he's learning his lesson. His family thinks that the world revolves around them. That they don't have no laws they have to abide to. And I keep telling him, "You have to follow rules and regulations. Things don't just come to you."

Then, too, I know they thought nobody would stick behind me, as far as my grandmother was concerned. They thought she wouldn't help me. And I kinda believed that in the beginning myself, until my grandmother did start. Because at the beginning, like I told her, "Gramma, you know Sylvia is out to take my child from me." "Oh, no, Leticia, she would never do that to you." She told me that when I was in the rehab. And even before that, when Terry was born, nobody believed me that they wanted him. Not until now.

But I knew it was true. Sylvia has some kind of fixation that makes her want my child. And the way I feel, she has nieces and nephews who need more help than Terry. More attention and caring. Her oldest sister, Darlene, has six kids and two grandkids. She's like thirty-six years old now, and the youngest grandchild's two and a half, so she could help them. And she could have her own! She's had abortions, so she *could* have more of her own kids. I guess she thinks this would make an already made family for her. And, too, I guess 'cause, like, this is Terrence's firstborn, and being that it's a boy, she wants him.

And she tried before to take away her own sister's youngest son. But her sister told her it's not going to happen. And Terrence's two older sisters, they both told me, "Leticia, Sylvia is out to get Terry from you." They said that 'cause she thinks I'm too young to be able to take care of him. And I says, "Listen, you know how many girls is out there younger than me!"

So now my gramma is very upset about the whole situation, 'cause when I was in rehab I had a letter drawn up stating that I wanted Terry to stay with her until I came home. But Sylvia would not give Terry to her, 'cause Sylvia said, "Terry's being toilet trained, and he's being weaned off his bottle." And Terry still drinks a bottle when he goes over there, and he wets his bed every night, even though he's almost four. But at the time, my grandmother was still working. She was getting ready to retire, so she said, "All right, let him stay there."

Then when I did get out of rehab they wouldn't let me see him, until one time. Terrence did let me take him for a weekend. It was a Sunday night, and I remember I was supposed to have him back. Well, I figured let him stay over one more day, till Monday. But no! At three o'clock in the morning, me, my mother, my stepfather, my brother, and my son are asleep. *Bang!* The police rap on the door. When my stepfather answered it, it was Sylvia and her son Shane coming through the door. So I got Terry up and they handed me a summons to come to court. I didn't think they would never do something like this. But it happened. And now here I am, going to court. I'm gonna regain custody of my son.

But the thing that really bothers me now is I see how upset Terry is about all this separation stuff. He's confused.

He tells me he wants to be with his father. He'll say, "I miss my daddy. Is he going to pick me up at school tomorrow?" And sometimes I'll get so mad at him 'cause he keeps askin' me that so often, until I says, "Terry, no! Your father's not picking you up today. He will be pickin' you up on Friday." And he repeats what I say. So now I'm trying to get him to know the days of the week. Every morning I wake up and say, "What's today, Terry?" And he doesn't know, so I say, "It's Wednesday," or whatever, so he knows that it isn't Friday.

Then, too, at other times he'll say, "Daddy says you're all bad. That he's gonna send the cops after you." Or he'll ask me, "Is Daddy and you gonna marry?" And I have to tell him no, that there's no chance of us ever getting back together, 'cause we just don't get along. But Terry surprises me so when he talks. He says things like, "I'm sorry that you all can't get back together. I love my daddy and I love my mommy too."

So this morning I went to court. I got up at five-thirty and doodled around the house. Then I took Terry to school. I had our things ready the night before, so all we had to do is wash up and get dressed. Gramma Rena came with me, and I took Hazela. At ten o'clock we went up to the fifth floor of Family Court, and in came Terrence, his stepfather, his mother, his aunt, and his nephew. I had a grin on my face in order to keep from getting upset or mad. I was playing with Hazela.

There we all sat, waiting and waiting. At a quarter to four in the afternoon, our lawyer came over to us to tell me I was going to regain total custody of Terry. The SPCC [Society for the Prevention of Cruelty to Children] talked them into it. So the only problem left was visitation rights. I told Terrence and his family what I wanted. Which they wouldn't honor. I told Terrence he could have him three weekends out of every month. But he wants him, or rather his sister wants Terry, every weekend. She's the one who did all the talking to me. But she has nothing to do with it. It's between the father and me. And they want him alternate holidays and three weeks out of every year. So I said no to it all. "We're gonna have to compromise," I told them. They can have him every other holiday, alternating years.

The whole court scene was too much. By the time the judge called us, we hadn't come to any conclusion, 'cause Terrence just sits there. Doesn't say nothing. And he was crying. But how am I supposed to feel? I don't care. I really don't. Not for him. All I said to myself was, Good. He deserves it! He put me through this nonsense. When November 8, 1986, came, they gave my son's custody to his aunt. I felt like part of me was taken away. You think anyone turned to me and comforted me? No. They could care less.

Justice was done. That's what I feel. My circumstances have changed. I'm not the person that I used to be. There's this saying I learned when I was in my rehab. "I'm not the woman I should be. I'm not the woman I could be. But thank God, I'm not the woman I used to be." And that's how I feel. Things have changed. This is just something that he's gonna have to realize. I'm not the girl that he met five years ago. So I think it's time for him to grow up and realize that a person can change for the better.

But underneath, I'll tell you, I do feel sorry for Terrence. I know this hurts him. But why should I think about his feelings? He put hisself in this position. When I had custody of Terry at the beginning, his father could visit him anytime he wanted. Terry was over there just about every weekend. I don't feel that anybody should put any *laws* as to when my child can see his father or not. And I know that Terrence is gonna come to my home one day and I'm gonna tell him how I feel. I'm just gonna tell him, "I really thought it was uncalled for. All this aggravation over the court thing. It was very unnecessary."

And I know, too, that Terrence is going to be very disappointed about the visitation arrangement. But we all have disappointments in our lives. Then, too, I know that this is not his doing. I know his sister and his mother's putting him up to this. And that's why I get mad at him. He doesn't listen to the things I tell him. "You are grown," I say to him. "Nobody can make decisions for you." But it goes in one ear and out the other. You tell him to do the right thing, and then he acts stupid. So I feel sorry for him.

And I think he notices that I don't depend on him the way I did at one time. I don't ask him for anything. No money. I don't even ask him to come see me. And I think that's something he misses.

And I feel he sees another change. I'm twenty years old now. Not sixteen or fourteen, like when he first met me. I talk to him different. Before, I didn't know what I was talking about. I didn't know as much then as I do now about a lot of things. I didn't know nothing about court.

And besides that, I also trusted people more. I'd just jump right into the first thing I'd see. I did what anybody wanted me to do. Now it's different. I'm trying to be more aware of what's going on around me. I'm more cautious. And I think he notices that. And you know, I dress differently too. I used to be more of a tomboy. I wore sneakers, like I was *hard*. Like I was bad! But now I dress more like a lady, like I'm supposed to be. Womanly.

It hurts. Me and Terrence have been through a lot together. He was the first person I told what happened to me with my stepfather. And that's why I can't understand his reasons for doing all this to me now. I feel a kind of disappointment in him.

But I'm thinking about calling him tonight. I just don't know. Most likely I won't, because either I'll be busy doing something else or I won't have the time. I really want to talk to him, though, to find out why it is that he can't take care of his own business. It must be something that they're saying to him. Or doing. That's why he can't say anything. I know me and him could talk. But maybe I should talk to him after this visitation thing is over. Maybe I should.

JULY 17    Well, I moved into my apartment, and I love it. I live on 132nd Street now. It's another apartment my grandmother owns. East 132nd. Apartment 5L, L as in Leticia! My apartment is big. Three rooms. One bedroom where the kids sleep. A living room I could section off to make another room. A kitchen. And I have a terrace. It's a beautiful area—I mean besides the other things that go on there. But my side of the street is beautiful. Secure. There's a doorman and I have an intercom, so nobody comes up unless he rings me first. The shopping area is right around the corner, and the washer and dryer is in the building, so I don't really have to go far. Except for school, I stay home all the time now. Sit on my terrace. I'm trying to get myself together.

I thought about not moving out of Queens, 'cause things were going well for me there. But just to have my freedom again. To be a little more responsible for myself. I feel better getting up in the morning. Going out. Taking Terry to school and paying my bills. I feel more responsible for me and my kids. And my nana was happy that I finally got on my feet again. Though I guess she didn't really want me to move out, 'cause I had the kids. A new baby in the house.

Me and my grandmother split the rent. It's $450 a month. But it's worth it. And I get public assistance. Only for myself, though. I'm going to court for child support, so I was told not to put them on welfare. Let Terrence pay the child support he owes. If they're on public assistance, then his money will be deducted from the money I get. Right now, though, he's not paying anything for them. That's why I have to go to court for the money.

Altogether, I get $362 and $45 worth of food stamps. And I get my WIC [Women, Infants and Children] checks every month. I bring them to the supermarket and I get eight thirteen-ounce cans of formula. And they give me checks for baby cereal and juice. When Hazela gets old enough to start eating food, they'll give her regular whole milk, cereal, cheese, peanut butter, eggs. I started with WIC when Terry was born.

And my grandmother helps me a lot. She comes to the apartment every day, 'cause she knows I'm at school. She may cook dinner for me, or she'll stay over the night and help out with the kids. I have a lot of support from her. So it's no problem. We're making it. I think sometimes, God forbid if anything would happen to her. What would I do?

And I've learned a big lesson! Already I lost a couple of friends. When they found out I had this apartment, they started saying, "Oh, I'm gonna come over and spend the night." But I told them, "Oh, no you're not!" Only if they have their own place and maybe they come over to visit with their baby and it's too late to go home. I have my kids! And I respect them now. I don't want everybody coming in and out of my home, giving them a bad impression about me. Won't be none of that this time.

And, too, I'm feeling good about my children. Terry is very intelligent. Very smart. He says what's on his mind. He tickles me so when he speaks. He sounds like a little ol' man. Like the other day, we were taking the bus to his school, and he said, "Oh, by the way, I'm sick of buses and subways. When can we start taking cabs?" He makes me laugh. Where does he get these phrases, "by the way"?

Although it's funny about Terry—even though he is my son, I don't feel that closeness to him that I do to Hazela. I treat him the same way. I play with him and talk to him. But I don't feel that close with him, 'cause he was with them for so long. With Hazela I know I'm doing the right things as far as she's concerned. I have the feeling she's mine. That I'm bringing her up myself. Even though my grandmother is helping me.

**SEPTEMBER 16**    The news of the day! I won my case in court. Thank God. No going back for my son anymore. The judge decided that I would get custody of Terry and that his father would get visitation three weekends in the month, every other holiday, and three weeks out of the year for vacation time. So I agreed upon it, and they were upset—Terrence, his sister, his mother. They all wanted custody of him. And they didn't want Terry to be with me. They tried to say I was an unfit mother. But they had no proof. You know, the funny thing is I really feel that being pregnant with Hazela saved me with getting my son back. You know how you have urine tests done, blood tests when you're pregnant? Well, they all had came out negative for drugs. So that was a strike for me. And they couldn't say that I was unfit, because I *did* go into rehab. Even though I just stayed for that one month.

So now I just have to go back to court in November for Hazela. Just to establish paternity. And that's gonna be another headache. Terrence's gonna make a big issue of it. He's gonna try and fight to say that this is not his daughter, even though we did take the blood test and I'm almost positive that when the results come back they will prove it. He did tell me, though, if she is his daughter he will take care of her. But I don't believe him. I mean I don't believe that he would do it on his own without me having to take him to court for child support. 'Cause I don't get nothing from him or those people now. I take care of my son by myself and my daughter. So first I have to establish paternity for Hazela. Then the public assistance lawyer will take him to court for child support for both children.

But I'll tell you this: if Terrence is gonna say anything that I set him up to get me pregnant, he has to have proof. If he feels he's not the father, that someone else is, he has to bring that person in. But he doesn't have proof. Truthfully, I don't even know if he believed me that I said I was using birth control. I can never figure him out. He's seen my pills before. It's not like he never seen them. But then, too, if he didn't believe me he could have used a condom. But he doesn't like them. He could say in court, though, "I protected myself, so I don't see why it's my fault." But anybody could say that they protected themself. The bag could break. You know what I'm saying?

I feel, though, that sooner or later he's gonna give in. Stop the charade with this court battle. 'Cause after a while, it's just aggravation. I'm fed up. I'm gonna be in and out of court for the rest of these kids' lives unless he decides to stop and do what's right. I really don't see why he's making this paternity thing a big issue. I wouldn't bother with the courts but for my kids. It's not for me. It's for my children. I have no choice if I'm gonna get justice.

———

But aside from all this court stuff, things is going pretty well. My apartment is coming along. I got the bathroom done. The rug and my nice sky-blue shower curtain. And my tiles for my kitchen. My grandmother hired a guy who does her other apartment, and he came to do mine. And I just went to go pay down on my VHS and my color TV. The next thing is to get the wall-to-wall carpet. My grandmother's working part-time, and then with my check I get from welfare, we just put together whatever money is left that I don't need. I put it aside for the things that I want to have. We put our money together and we're taking our time getting things. It's coming out very nice.

And the kids are happy too. They're growing. Hazela is getting older. She's six months. And she's so active. She says "dada." She's doing patty-cake. She walks in her walker and stands up in her crib. She's doing everything early, the doctor says. So I'm trying to keep up with her. But she's moving too fast for me. The two of them together. I'm surprised I'm surviving.

My mother, though, she takes Hazela on some weekends. Usually if I go out one evening, she'll take her till the next day. She comes over to my apartment now. Stays for a while and we talk. Me and my mother have been really progressing together as far as communicating, because for a long time I couldn't say a word to her. Nothing concerning my problems, 'cause we'd end up arguing. But now, even before I moved in here, she said, "We have to meet each other halfway. If you have any problems, you come talk to me, and if I have anything that I don't like that you're doing, I'll tell you about it." Now that I'm older, we can relate a little better.

But I'd probably be a loony tune by now without my grandmother! Many times I almost felt like I was going to reach that cliff and jump.

We go back to court November 6. That's when they'll decide paternity. And this morning I was on a bus, daydreaming that everything came out positive. That they told Terrence he had to take care of this child. He was just devastated 'cause he didn't want to believe that this is his daughter. He was shocked. And I was happy. I was really laughing!

Soon it will all be over, all this paternity business. And anyway, I have a new boyfriend! LeRoy. I've known him for three weeks. I haven't really told anybody, because I want to give it some time. See that we're really together. But this time, I'm rocking the cradle! He's nineteen, almost two years younger than I am. But he's intelligent, and we get along. He makes me happy.

**OCTOBER 7**    I've been at this Y for too long! I feel like I'm just sitting here. Doing nothing. And the years go by. I'll be twenty-one years old in November. I've been here at the Y since I was sixteen, off and on. I say to myself, when am I ever going to go and take my test for my diploma? I have this apartment, and I want to furnish it nice. I would like to get a job.

But I tell you, my mind is somewhere else. Trying to find a way for me to go and get some money. I think about my kids. The things they need. My mind's not concentrating. And I feel very uncomfortable. I'm the oldest girl here. Last year a lot of girls had just started the program, and they went to take their GED and passed it. And now they're gone.

I haven't taken my GED in two years. Last year when I was pregnant with Hazela, I was on maternity leave for like four months. And the first time I took the test, I had such a negative attitude. I just knew I wasn't gonna pass it. And me and my friend, we took this stuff, some drug that made us laugh a lot, so I couldn't keep my mind on it. But I only missed it by eighteen points. The highest mark is 350, but 225 is passing. I got 207.

Now, though, my teacher at the Y says to me, "Whatever work I give you, I'll give you a test and you'll never pass it. You're not near taking that test." So that got me real upset. "You mean to tell me the whole time I've been here since last year and I haven't been close to passing it? How would you know?" I asked her. "You haven't tested me to find out where I'm at!" And she just says that all this work should be a review for me. And she's right. But my thoughts are not on my work. I'm thinkin' about my life. My kids.

I'm going to take this test on my own, though. There's a building on 125th Street where they give it. So I'll bring my results from my other test and my Social Security card, and just do it. They can't stop me. And I also requested that maybe the Y could get me into another program, where I'll go to college and get credits toward my high school diploma. I think they have a program like that at Roberto Clemente College in the Bronx. But like I said, I'm getting very impatient. I want to move on. Only thing is, I don't think they want me to leave now. I guess I influence the other girls to do things positively. And that's what the girls need in the program. And a lot of girls look up to me 'cause I say what's on my mind. I'm their leader. And I kinda feel good about that, 'cause I used to be a follower.

And I'd miss my counselor here. I don't run to Della for

every little thing like I used to. Now I go to her when it's a problem like court or things I can't handle. She gives me advice. But for little problems, like my boyfriend, I can handle those myself. So I would miss her. But I feel that once I stop seeing Della, I done stepped up the ladder one step. And I'd be more independent. And I've always liked my independence. I remember my mother used to say—and I used to feel bad about this—"You're not grown until you're eighteen. Whatever I say goes in this house." I felt I was being held back from the things I wanted to do. Then, when I got on my own, I was like, Good. I can do whatever. I can stay up late. 'Cause I always wanted to know what happens after five o'clock, since I was in the house so much. But then I started going out at night. And it was nothing! Just dark. That's all. Everything that happens during the day just about is happening at night. Or maybe worse, you know. So all my party stuff, it just kinda died down. I didn't want to do it no more. There's a time to get serious.

All I'm doing is seeing this guy LeRoy. He works on Fifty-seventh Street, where Terry goes to school. I met him when I left Terry off there one morning. LeRoy was going in the opposite direction, and he said, "My God, you're a healthy woman!" So I had to say, "I know." And then I kept walking. But then when I got to the Y he had followed me, and he said, "Come here." So he asked me my name. And when I told him, he said, "I would like to come see you." And I had to tell him that I didn't think it was such a great idea, 'cause I had just met him.

When I meet someone, I don't like to bring them to my home right away. I hear from my grandmother. So it took maybe two weeks—no, one week—before he came to my place. But I got to know him 'cause I see him every day when I take Terry to school. I know what time he has to be to work. So I'm there exactly that time.

And we're trying to work things out. He's been with the kids. He gets along with them. And Terry is like real happy having a man in the house. The other night when LeRoy came over, Terry was smiling and laughing the whole time. Really enjoying himself. And LeRoy called me last night. All he keeps telling me is, "I love you. I love you." He says, "I'm never gonna leave you, and you don't leave me." That's all he ever talks about. This weekend I want to take him to the Hard Rock Café. I love it there. It's so noisy, and you can have a Tequila Sunrise, a big juicy steak and potatoes. The works! We take turns payin'. And you know, he's lucky, 'cause I've never treated a man to nowhere.

When I go out with guys now, I'm very cautious with who I associate with. It used to be so easy for me to fall into a trap. Now I interrogate them. I go through twenty-one questions. Who was the last girl you was intimate with? When was the last time you was with a girl? All those questions. I mean I go through it. I have to have proof they're OK. I've got so that I can read a person when I first meet them. Sometimes I'm kinda fooled 'cause they can put up a front so well. But then I can read in between the lines. Actions speak louder than words. And I have to meet their family. My grandmother says, "You know how a man is by his family."

I haven't met LeRoy's family yet, though. He says his grandmother . . . He lives with both his grandparents, and one has leukemia and the other has cancer. He lives with them in a senior citizens' building, and he's not supposed to be there. So I told him, "OK, but I want to meet your father." He lives out on Long Island. So I will. And time will tell.

And I'm careful these days. I carry condoms too. Men don't like to use them. But I encourage them, 'cause I don't want to die. I want to live, and nobody's gonna admit to "I have AIDS." They're not gonna tell you that. That's what makes it so bad about being intimate, 'cause you have to choose life or death. It took two weeks before LeRoy agreed to use a condom. I said, "Well, if you're not going to use it, you're not going to have it." So he came to agree. And I use the pill too, ever since I had Hazela. But I've always kept condoms, even before I heard about AIDS, 'cause there's all those other venereal diseases. But right now, it's bad. That's why I'm not into too many guys. I'm afraid I may catch a bad disease. And what would happen to my kids? How's their future gonna be without me?

My bottom line is now I don't wanna get hurt, and I'm lookin' out for me! And I told LeRoy, "If you hurt me, you're gonna feel it." I don't like nobody to play with my emotions. I'm very sensitive when it comes to telling somebody about my feelings. Putting my feelings out there.

**OCTOBER 15**   The way I look at it, I got a good side to my family and a bad side. My mother's side I feel is up to par. My father's is down-up. I'm not in that side. I'm over here in the good situation, 'cause I've been with my mother's side of the family ever since I've known. I don't even know too much about my father's family and where they're from.

I know that my father's mother had seven kids of her own. And she's raising another seven, 'cause her oldest daughter died and she had four daughters. And her other daughter's not doing so hot now from drugs either. So that makes another three. And her youngest son, Greg, her baby, he's in prison. You know how you can spoil a child so much that they just expect a whole lot? That they have to go commit a crime to get what they want? That's what happened to him. He used to rob this store on 100th Street constantly. The *same* store. Now I feel, if you're gonna do it, you do it right! I get on his case. He calls me from prison and we talk.

And then, too, he was jumpin' his parole and went out and robbed again. So they gave him three to seven years about three years ago. And he's got two daughters now, 'cause he got married in jail. And his wife is having another baby. And they've broke up.

I tell myself I'll slap myself before I get into a situation like that. I feel, OK, he's my uncle, but on her part, I couldn't do it. She's living at home with her parents in a not big apartment at all. All her brothers and sisters still live there, and they're grown.

And with my father, like he's got his problems too. Drugs. And he's the same old muleheaded person he always was. I went to visit him in the Bronx. He lives across the street from his mother. And he talked to me the way he always did. With the same kind of tone. Nothing personal. Just, "What are you doin' with yourself? You still in school?"

He likes to run other people's lives. He still likes to tell me what to do. But he knows, ever since that time we got into that argument, he's not gonna run *my* life. We got into it about four years ago, when he went to Washington, D.C. He told me he was going to let me have his apartment, 'cause he was getting a house down there. So I was at his place with my two half-sisters and my half-brother. Terry was about six months. And he called one day at around three in the afternoon, and I wasn't there to be with his two kids when they came home from school. And then one kid answered the phone and said, "Oh, she's just walking in now."

So when I picked up the phone he said to me, "What the fuck you doin' not being at the house on time!" And I was burned, 'cause my father never spoke to me like that before. I tried to explain that I had to go downtown to pick up my check, and all he said was, "I don't care about your check!" So we had words, and he told me to "get the hell out of my house." And I did. And ever since then I stand up to him and let him know he can't tell me what to do. And I had never stood up to my father before that time. I was always afraid of him, 'cause he had that big, fatherly image. You say the wrong word, you'll get slapped. Even though my father never hit me.

So now I get back at him whenever I can. I retaliate! When I go to visit his mother, I bring Hazela and I leave her there. Then I go drop in on my father. If he asks me to bring the baby to see him, I say yes, but I don't do it. I just leave and don't come back. He promises me things and he never comes through. So why should I?

The only good thing on my father's part is his independence. He knows how to take care of business. He's business-oriented. And he's had a number of them. Construction maintenance, contracting, cleaning service for blinds and rugs, a satellite business, for those things you put on top of buildings. Only problem is, he doesn't like paying people who work for him. And, too, every business he's had always reaches the top and then for some reason they just go downhill. But he can create his own invention of a business. That's what I adore about him. He's independent, not like my mother. She's the type who needs someone to cling on, to help guide her. And me, I could do it on my own. Like him. I don't need nobody to help me. If I get up and go out there and get it, I'm gonna get it myself. I don't need somebody sitting and holding my hand. Showing me the ropes. That's how my mother is. But my father just goes out there and does it. So in that way I look up to him.

**OCTOBER 22**    Well, my birthday's next month. November 23. And I want an erotic cake! No, two cakes. One of the female organ and one of the male. But for a hundred dollars I'm not getting it. I have to buy a regular one.

I'll be twenty-one. I'm getting old. Getting up there. The way I feel, there's not much more for me to see. I've been through everything. I don't say I have nothing to look forward to. I have my kids growing up. They're having a good time. But for me, I'm just gonna be a working girl. Find me a job. 'Cause, personally, I'm not gonna be on welfare too long.

———

The other day we had a press conference with a lot of New York City politicians, and a bunch of us girls talked about welfare and working, increasing the minimum wage and more training programs. And we talked about rents and loans for colleges. A lot of girls were talking about having our own apartment. That we don't get enough welfare for rent and that rent should be lowered so we can live and begin our own homes. We all said that we want public assistance to come to us, not our parents, who collect it now till we're over eighteen. The way I feel is why should parents get money for a teenager who *is* a mother? She's the one who had the child, and that's her responsibility. So why not give her the money to take care of the baby? Personally, I did get welfare money when I was fifteen, 'cause I wasn't living at home with my mother. And I didn't have a relative who was taking care of me all the time. You can get it if you lie and tell them you don't live with nobody. Then you're considered "emancipated." They don't know, and they don't check too well.

The way I feel about welfare is I'm not on welfare to depend on welfare. I feel it's just something temporary until I'm able to go and get me a job. I mean it's kind of hard not to depend on it, if you don't have money. But people make welfare seem so bad. I don't know why, but I don't feel it is. It's something to help you out for the time being until you're able to take care of yourself. It's true that there are some people who sit and wait for checks, who stay on welfare for years. But a lot of them do have children, and you can stay home until your child is six years old. Until your child goes to school and then you can go to work.

Then, too, I feel that I have worked. I have had taxes taken out of my paycheck. So I'm only getting my taxes back. Like I was a messenger at PaineWebber. I worked there for about three months. Then I moved on to Checkers restaurant, and I was a waitress there, working behind a counter for a month or so. Then I went to work at Cosmopolitan Temporary Agency, and I got work as a cashier at another restaurant. But at that time I was pregnant with Hazela, and they fired me 'cause I was so tired. I'd come in late from oversleeping in the morning. I was so tired from being pregnant. All the other jobs I quit 'cause they were summer jobs and I was going back to school.

Right now, my mother's talking about a job for me working for VISTA [Volunteers in Service to America]. It's full-time. But she tells me I could go to night school. I think that's what I'm gonna do. And I'd be working with homeless people, placing them in different programs. I'd get paid $466 a month. And it doesn't interfere with public assistance. They take $75 out of my monthly paycheck for twelve months, and you sign a contract saying that you'll work for them for a year. At the end of that time they give you that money back. I would like a job like that. I like to hear about other people's lives. I'm very curious. And, too, I feel that these people need people to talk to. They need someone they can trust.

But I'm not gonna look into that job now. I just want to concentrate on the paternity thing. I still don't really know who Hazela's father is. But everybody thinks it's Terrence. I can't wait till the decision, in two weeks. Gavin is coming to court, and so is Terrence. They'll both be so nervous in the back of the room. And I'll be kinda happy. I'll be grinning 'cause I know that this is something Terrence doesn't want. And in some ways I don't want it either, 'cause I know he really don't want Hazela. But if she is his daughter, he has no choice but to take care of her.

Right now Terrence is starting to take care of Terry, buying him clothes, 'cause we had a confrontation the other day on the phone. And we were talking about getting back together. And I told my girlfriends this, and they said, "If you go back with him, we'll never talk to you again after what he put you through." But I said, "Maybe so, but if that's both my kids' father, then I feel that I can kinda understand." I don't blame him for everything that's happened. I won my custody case, and it was more or less his mother's and sister's fault what was going on. I don't really ridicule him for all the things they wanted.

And you know, I really miss Terrence. I haven't been with him for so long. Way more than a year. And things are different. I have values and morals, and I really think about them. I feel that I wouldn't do the same things that I done before, 'cause I've learned from those things. I think this time we both learned. But I think it's gonna take him some time to really start trusting me again, because of the things that I've done. But I mean it was done years past. I'm not taking drugs no more.

And now when we talk on the phone, I can tell Terrence everything. Even who I'm seeing. We both are able to communicate and tell what's on each other's mind. That's what was missing before. We had to hide our feelings and hide the things that we were doing from each other. And I think that now that we've been separated for some time, we're able to talk about his girlfriend or whoever he's seeing or me with whoever I'm seeing. We even talk about sex. We haven't had intercourse, but we do talk about it.

I know, too, that if we got back together I could accept that he was seeing another girl. I don't have a jealous bone in my body over one man. And that took some doing, because I used to be one jealous girl! But now it don't bother me, 'cause if he really cares about me, why should I worry? He's with me. At least he would be honest enough to tell me he's seeing someone. Like LeRoy, he keeps bringin' up excuses about why he can't see me. "I'm sick. I can't come over." I haven't seen him three times in three weeks. But it don't bother me. What LeRoy's doing, he can do, 'cause Leticia's gonna do what she wants to.

I know I can't live with Terrence. We both know that. But if he asked me to marry him, I would. But only on one condition. He'd stay where he's at and I'd stay where I'm at. We just don't belong in the same house. We argue too much. And I like to do my thing. Like when I come home, I throw my clothes around. He does it too. But it may take me three days to go around my house and pick them up. And he'll be coming in from work and say, "Leticia, you ain't washed my clothes." Leticia this, Leticia that. I can't live like that. I hate it. I don't want to take care of him in these ways. I just want to go out and have fun. And I want to say, "This is my husband." We'd do things together. If he wanted to come over and spend the night, he could, but I would not go to his house.

So when we talked, he said maybe we could hang out together. Nothing serious. A dinner. The movies. When he has time, he said, he'd call me.

**NOVEMBER 19**    Terrence is not Hazela's father. I went down to Family Court. It was just me alone, and Terrence came with his niece. The judge said the test was negative. "Terrence Brown is not the said father of Hazela." My lawyer then said that we were withdrawing the petition. I didn't even look Terrence's way. He flew out the door as soon as he heard it. My lawyer asked who the father was. I didn't bother to tell him, 'cause I didn't want any more of these hassles.

That night I saw Gavin, who is the father. His whole attitude changed. At the beginning of all this, he said, "If it's my child, I'll help you pay for stuff." But now he just said, "You wanted a child. You kept her. Now it's your child." He also asked me for proof that it is his child, but I don't want anything to do with him anymore. Unfortunately, it just had to be like this. Maybe it's for the better. He's not ready to take care of her anyway. Only thing I'm upset about is that Hazela won't know her father. When she comes to me asking, what will I tell her?

When I think about Terrence, I think I despise him. Though sometimes I have mixed feelings. I dream that I'm gonna get him back. That we'll be together again. But I'm doing OK without him. In fact, I'm doing better. So I think to myself that I don't need him back.

But I broke up with LeRoy too. He's silly. He doesn't know what he wants to do with his life. I have things that I want to do. I have places to go. And I don't want him just hanging around. He acts like he wants to be a messenger his whole life. And besides, he didn't come to my birthday. I turned twenty-one years old, and it was a night I'll never forget. I had made *three* cakes before one came out right. They kept falling in. I was so mad. But in the end it was delicious. Everybody ate all the cake. I didn't even get a piece, it was that good!

And there was a lot of people. I invited thirty kids, but there was about fifty. Even the police came, 'cause the music was too loud. But luckily my girlfriend's boyfriend's a cop, and he was there, so there was no problem. The policeman even gave me a kiss on the cheek and wished me Happy Birthday. Just the DJ was late. He said he'd come at nine, but he came at eleven. But after that I was so zonked drunk, I don't remember too much. My brother brought me Amaretto. I had Bacardi, Gold Reserve, blackberry brandy. I didn't drink all of that. I just gave it to everybody and told them to have fun.

Then, at like five o'clock Sunday morning, one of the girls that was there said she got her leather coat stolen. But I know for a fact she didn't have no leather coat when she arrived. They were trying to skin me for $235. But I told her I wasn't paying, so they left me alone.

But everybody came. And that was the biggest present for me. Everybody showing up and celebrating my birthday with me. Just not LeRoy. And my brother celebrated with me too.

And that made me very happy, 'cause we haven't been together in a while. Vernon's nineteen now, and he was the life of the party! He made everybody get up and dance. He took control of it and kept everything in order. I felt close to him. I kind of depend on my brother for some of my happiness. He brightens my day. When I'm down and gloomy, he makes me laugh. And all the girls love Vernon. It's really just me and my brother anyway. I mean my parents never gave us much, so I'm glad we have each other.

Know what my father did for my birthday? Nothing. Now, with my mother, I don't expect her to call, although she does call on my birthday. She never says happy birthday. She just sort of says, "Well, how does it feel to be, like, twenty-one?" When I got up in the morning, I sort of waited for her to call. And I was thinking all day, Why doesn't she call? Then later in the day, at the end of it, she called to say hello.

But my father, now that's a different story. He has no excuses. Like with my mother and her being a Jehovah's Witness, she's kind of weird about things. So if she doesn't do anything about my birthday, I don't care. But my father, like when it's his birthday, every year I call him. I visit him. I buy him a present. But he doesn't appreciate it. Somehow I keep thinking my father is gonna call. But he never does.

The only trouble I had over my birthday was with my grandmother. She was mad because I was having a party. "You can't afford it. You don't have the money," she'd keep saying. But I didn't let that stop me. I just acted macho with her. "I'm having it anyway," I told her. I'm able to talk to my grandmother in any way whatever. I don't disrespect her, but if I'm angry, she knows I'm angry. I don't be sweet with nobody, unless it's called for. I'm not gonna sit down and say, "Listen, Gramma, I would like to have this party 'cause of such and such a reason." No! If I want something, I want it. And I want it now. I don't take my time saying something.

And my grandmother's really gettin' on my nerves lately. I'm getting older, and I'm not needing her anymore. And all these guys are calling and she says, "I don't know who they are." I don't tell her much now, 'cause I feel things are private. And besides, I don't want her to stop me from doing what I want. If I have no money, I don't ask her for much. Maybe carfare. Something like that. But she wants me to get a part-time job. With me in school, though, and having the kids, and now Terry has the chicken pox and Hazela has her earache . . . I know that public assistance don't give you enough, but it's really hard to look for a job right now.

Anyway, when my grandmother gave me the apartment at first, the agreement was that I pay some rent, the telephone, and Con Ed, and she would come over like once a week. Now she's here every day. And she keeps complaining, "Leticia, do this. Do that." I can't stand hearing about all the bad things, the dreary things she dreams up. It makes me want to go to sleep. She's always talking about problems. I want life to be soothing, comfortable. Full of laughs.

I know she's having a hard time maintaining her bills. My apartment and hers. That's why she's taking in kids now. She has five babies she cares for every day at my place. She wants to furnish the apartment, she says. But I didn't ask her to do that. Though she acts as if I did. She tells me I'm not appreciative. She says I want my cake and eat it too. And that's sort of true. I am a dreamer sometimes. But I don't promise things to my kids that I know I can't give them. Like I wanted an answering machine, and she got real mad. "You're always spending money on things, your VHS, your stereo. But I tell her, "Well, it's my money!" But then sometimes I have to ask her for carfare or a box of Pampers.

It's just that I can't get used to somebody's giving me advice. I feel like I've always been independent. I've done things on my own. And I can't stand her picking and nagging. Especially about the guys I see. She thinks I'm gonna go back to what I was before. A hooker. 'Cause one time Vernon said, "I saw you, Leticia. Out on Park Avenue and 116th Street with a turquoise top and bottom." And that's where all the prostitutes stand around. And my grandmother heard him say that, and she believed him. But it wasn't me.

So now I keep this little appointment book, which I would never let her see. I keep everything in there. All the names of guys. The money I owe for the VHS. When my bills are due. I keep my whole life in this book. If she ever saw all the guys' names in there, she'd think I am what I used to be. But I'm not. Since that episode, though, I always say where I am in my book, so that if anybody thinks differently, I have proof.

Anyway, I'm gonna surprise my gramma today. I passed my eleventh-grade city test. So I'll be taking my GED pretty soon. And passing that too!

**DECEMBER 2**     Today's Hazela's ninth month into this world. I wish we'd never have to get older. Once you do, you start to realize things. Some things that you don't when you're a baby, 'cause then you're all about having fun. Sometimes I wish I were nine months old. I want somebody to do it for me. To care for me. I wouldn't have to take on any responsibilities.

I had my Thanksgiving alone this year. Just me and Terry and Hazela. It was quiet. Nobody called me. I didn't do nothing. Just stayed home. I loved it. Peace and silence. Nobody bothering me. 'Cause if I had gone somewhere, it would have been noisy and I'd probably be aggravated at the end of the day. I would have wanted to go to bed. I was expecting my girlfriend to come over. But she didn't. And she didn't call. I made boneless chicken breasts. My babies like that.

My grandmother had Thanksgiving with my aunt and her family. And my brother—he was supposed to come over, but he made me mad because he didn't. He went over to everybody else's house. And I told him that I kinda felt that his friends were more important than me. That he spent more time with them than his own sister. But he told me it wasn't true. "Don't I always find you wherever you're at?" he said to me. "Truth is," I told him, "that don't mean nothing. You find me. I'm here. But do you spend any time with me?"

I'm all tired out today. I have nothing to say. Only thing is that this morning we went to this panel, to talk to teenagers from nine schools in New York City. They wanted us to talk about teenage pregnancy and drugs. I just hope that I got across to one of them. I hope that it'd be helpful in their life to hear about young mothers. Having children at such a young age when you really haven't established yourself . . . It's like everybody says, it's not easy. And that is true. And I gave the example like now of having Terry. If I would have thought back before I had him about what he's gonna want for Christmas—'cause he's given me a list, and I know that right now I can't afford to give him certain things—then I probably wouldn't ever have had him.

I know I can't change the situation. I can't change that I do have him. And I was trying to talk to these kids, to prevent them from getting into a situation where a guy wants to have intercourse with them or vice versa. I told them that they'd have to make a decision. That they'd have to think about all the angles. But I know no one really thinks about the reality before you have intercourse. I mean, at that age, no one does.

Anyway, I'm tired of giving speeches. I'm the one they always ask. I don't know where they get this feeling from here, that I'm in charge or something. The leader. I don't feel that way. I guess maybe because I've been through a lot and I can express myself a little more than some of the girls here. The girls, like, they always want me to ask for something for the class, because I usually get it. You see I can talk. I'm a good conniver. I'll give good reasons. Some of them beat around the bush. I come straight to it. I know the ropes of getting what I want.

DECEMBER 10     Well, I got a job! I started working at Checkers today. It's a chicken and ribs store. I love it. It's where I used to work last summer. The summer of '86. Only thing is, I didn't want to drop out of school, but they kinda left me no choice. When I came into school this past Monday, I left Hazela and Terry with my grandmother. But they told me nobody can come to school without their children no more unless you got an appointment or something like that. So even if I work part-time in the afternoons, I still would have to bring Hazela to the Y with me. That means getting up maybe five-thirty or six in the morning, getting all three of us together. Feeding them. Then taking Terry to his school. When it would be time for me to go to work, I would have to take Hazela from the Y nursery, back home uptown. That's an hour's ride. Then go back downtown and go to work. I told them no. That's too much on me.

The other choice was for me to just stay in school and finish. That would be another year or so. So they said I could stay here in school or go to work and maybe they'd get me into a night school program. I told my counselor I'd take my test next month and I'd work now. I could use the extra money, especially now with Christmas.

And I got this job myself. I called up one of the managers from last year, and he said, "Come down." So I did, and now I pack deliveries. And I'm in the Wall Street area, so I'll be going all day. The phones don't stop, and it's crowded! The manager that's taking care of things now doesn't know that I can also answer the phones. So he'll probably let me do that too. I can do a few things at one time.

My hours are perfect: 10:00 A.M. to two-thirty. I get up

early. Hazela is my alarm. I get myself together, and I usually get Terry up at seven. I allow another fifteen minutes to feed him, and we leave at a quarter to eight. By the time I get him to school it's about nine o'clock. That leaves me an hour to get downtown. When we're off at work, I stay there to eat. We're allowed to do that. Then I just go pick Terry up. It works out all great for me. And Hazela loves being with the kids my grandmother takes care of. Only thing is, if I go to night school now, I have to get a baby-sitter for them. So I don't think I'll go right now. I just wanna work.

I get four dollars an hour to start with. Then they'll raise it a dollar. And I work six days a week. My grandmother's really happy I'm working, 'cause I'm always asking her for money. I'm the type to have things. I like expensive things. I have good taste. So she's been telling me, "Why don't you go out and get you a job and make your own money. Then you can do what you want with it. As long as you have to depend on somebody, you'll never be satisfied." So I got tired of hearing it over and over. And I got me a job.

And she was right too, 'cause I don't like to ask her for money. And like now when I ask her, I'm borrowing it. And she says, "I hope you're going to pay it back." But I can, because I get paid every Tuesday, so I will have money every week. And I won't even have to ask her. I won't have to worry about asking my grandmother for nothing.

# 11 ▪ *"What's the same is, I leave all the guys"*

## *Leticia Johnson*

**DECEMBER 17**    I have a friend now. He's not a boyfriend yet. Just a male friend. His name is Malcolm. And he's in prison. The only reason I got involved with him was through my uncle Delmont. He's in prison for extortion. I asked my uncle, "Any guys up there?" And he said, "There's a whole bunch of 'em." So I said, "No, I mean one in particular. One nice guy that you think I could talk to as a pen pal or something." At first he said no, but then he said, "Well, there is one." And I asked him to tell me about him. Because me and my uncle talk on the phone. It's not like what you see on television. Prisoners can talk to outsiders. Shows like "T. J. Hooker" or "Spenser: For Hire"—it makes prisons look bad. That's not really what it's like, being in prison.

I asked my uncle, "When I come visit you, do I talk to you on the phone or something? Or in a booth?" And he said, "No, we'll all be sitting around a table. I can touch you and hold your hand. You been watching too much television," he said.

———

But I've never been in prison, you know. Close to it, but not in. I don't know much about it, so I asked my uncle to describe some of the things people are in for. And he said, "Murder. Some of them are on death row." And I sit and listen. I'm interested. Curious. I want to find out how prison life is. What it looks like. Do you have to go through all these gates and guards like you see in the movies?

So I'm meeting with my uncle for the first time in ten years. He's twenty-seven. He's been there since he was seventeen or eighteen. But like I said, I've spoken to him before. He'll call when I'm at my grandmother Doreen's house, and I'd promise that I was gonna come visit. The thing is, once people find out that you're in prison, they rarely come see you. Like family or friends that you thought were your friends when you were on the outside, once you get in there, they don't want to be bothered with you. And I don't want my uncle to feel that I don't care about him.

And, too, a lot of things have been hidden from me and my brother on my father's side of the family, and I want to know about these things. So I want to ask my uncle. Like I just found out how my father's sister Regina died. My uncle told me that her youngest child's father gave her an overdose. And this child was born a week before she died. He's never seen his mother, nor his father. Doreen's been raising him from a baby for twelve years.

And I learned that Regina was her father's favorite child, so when she passed, he died, 'cause he used to be an alcoholic. And after having drunk so much and his daughter passing, it was too much strain on his heart. He had a heart attack.

And now my grandmother Doreen's not doing so great healthwise. Only one out of her seven children is helping her. Delmont's in prison, so he can't help. And my father and his two sisters, they're on drugs. On crack. And that really bothers me, about my father especially. He knows that

I was doin' bad when I was on them, and he was the one who took me to the hospital when I had got my arms broke. But hey, I have nothing to say. He leads his life. He knows what it will do to him. But it's one of the reasons that I don't visit him much. Or take the kids there.

My uncle Delmont got six to twelve years, like Malcolm. They're both up to go before the parole board in about a year and a half. And when I go there, my uncle's gonna introduce me to Malcolm in person. I've already written to him for a couple of weeks, and he's called me. He seems like he's a nice guy. But he hasn't told me why he's in there. I'm gonna ask him, though. And he will. I know he won't hold nothing back from me. He will say it. I'm that way too.

Like I told my uncle straight out, "I'm afraid to come up there. Suppose somebody just decides to hold me hostage? It could be a freak day or something. You never know." But he told me, "I'm not gonna ever let that happen to you." I says, "OK. But I'll tell you one thing. I'm gonna be looking behind my shoulder every five minutes, 'cause this is my first time in a prison."

JANUARY 7, 1988    Hazela's ten months now. She's walking. She's talking. She has four teeth. She says her own name. She says "Gramma." And she says "Hetha," the name of one of the little girls my grandmother takes care of. She's doing very good. We talk to her a lot. And now that she knows how to walk, she doesn't sit down for nothing.

Terry's more like his father. The boss of the house. The two of them get into it over toys. Hazela grabs him and smacks him, but he won't hit her back. He's doing good too. He loves school. Only thing, he's allergic to just about everything. And he's overactive. So I have to keep him home sometimes, 'cause he tires himself out, and he doesn't know when to sit down and he gets sick. I have to slow his pace sometimes.

He sees his father on weekends. Terrence picks him up

from school. I don't know why he's so interested in his son all of a sudden. But I'm not complaining.

Terrence and his sister and husband bought Terry a motorcycle for Christmas. A real one! It's got four wheels and a regular engine, so it doesn't even fit in the house. They're teaching him how to ride it. It's big enough for two adults. But what is he doing with a motorcycle? He's only four years old! Now all the other grandkids are jealous, 'cause they've never gotten things like this.

I don't know why they have this closeness to Terry. I guess 'cause Terrence is the youngest and the only boy and this is his son. But I'm not knocking it, 'cause some kids have and some kids don't have, you know.

JANUARY 10    Well, Malcolm *is* my boyfriend! I went to see him at the prison. He told me he's twenty-two years old. He's been in prison about seven years. On and off. He went in at fifteen. Then he came out at eighteen, and he went back in again for robbery. He wasn't even home that long before he went back.

They have this cabin before you go into the main part of the correctional facility. We stayed there for about five hours, talking. But before I met him, I was sitting there for about a half hour, waiting. And I was nervous. I kept dreaming that they were gonna hold me hostage and I wouldn't never be going home to my kids.

Then when I first seen him, I automatically knew it was him. I just had that feeling. He had described hisself to me. But that fit the description of a lot of guys walking in that door. Still, when he came and sat down, I was grinning. And he looked at me funny too. I was afraid to sit close to him, 'cause he's in there for attempted murder. He told me that over the phone. He said he had got into this fight with a guy and that Malcolm tried to kill the guy. And I was thinking, Oh, Lord, is he gonna kill me?

———

Man, he's exciting! I visit him three times a week. Wednesday, Saturday, and Sunday. It takes forty-five minutes by train from New York City. I love riding up there. And then talking to him from nine-thirty in the morning to quarter of four. We have a good time, talking and eating all day.

And he's funny. Certain things we discuss makes me laugh. Like he's been there for years and he hasn't had intercourse in a long time. So he may make a funny jest about it, and I'll laugh. And, too, I like him 'cause he's not like me in ways. He's more social, more outgoing.

And he's a good communicator. He talks to me, and that's something I always missed in a relationship. I need it. 'Cause he comes straight out. We don't bite our tongues if we have something to say. Like he says, "I'm gonna give it to you raw." I want that. That's the way I am too. 'Cause there are things I don't like about Malcolm, and I tell him. "You're too demanding. Too conceited." He does think he's God's gift to the world. That everything should come to him. He doesn't have to do anything for it. He has an attitude problem. Like he'll tell me, "I want you to do this. Come up on a certain day." When I tell him I have to work late, he says, "Why do you have to do that?" And he tells me, "I'm boss. I'm not changing for nobody. Nobody can make *me* change. I'm gonna be myself for the rest of my life."

But then, the way I feel, he's just putting up a macho front. 'Cause, see, in there, there's a certain way he has to act when he's around those other guys. If he don't, he looks bad. But I tell him, "Look, I'm not in there with you. I'm no inmate. I'm a woman, and I expect you to treat me differently." And sometimes he'll respond. If he says something on the phone I don't like, I'll hang up. And he'll call me back and say, "I'm sorry." But then he says he has the upper hand. He's gonna tell me what to do. But I says, "No you ain't. You gotta depend on me for everything, 'cause you're there and I'm here."

And I took Hazela up there three times already. Before he even seen her he said he loved her. And as long as he loves me, he loves Hazela too. As if she were his own. And he gave me some money for us, 'cause my telephone bill was three hundred dollars. He calls me collect almost every night. So he gave me five hundred dollars, and he told me to pay my telephone bill and my rent and whatnot. People would think he got his money from drugs, but he never dealt any drugs. His mother passed and left him and her other kids a certain amount of money, and his sister manages his. She put his in CDs.

His sisters sit and tell me about when he was a child. He was always troubled. Getting into things wrong. His mother tried to raise the four of them by herself, 'cause his father left when Malcolm was real young.

Malcolm says when he comes home in '90, he wants to get married. We wanted to get married now, but we both feel that now wouldn't be the right time. He don't want to make me feel that by him marrying me, it's only for his trailer visits. Like they go on trailer visits for three days. You're still on the grounds of the prison, but you live in a trailer. And since he's been in there for years, well, his being with me for three days! Imagine, OK? He don't just want to marry for intercourse. He wants to marry me 'cause he loves me. Because he wants to spend his life with me.

And that's what some of the girls do up there. They meet a guy and they're with him for two months and next thing they're married, 'cause the guy wanted to have pleasure. I don't want to marry a man because he wants to enjoy having sex. That'll always come into play. But marriage is more than just sex.

Anyway, right now, I don't know him well enough to marry him. I'm getting to know him. But I haven't seen no other guy . . . well, except for yesterday. But I have not gone to bed with another guy in about a month. I'm not dating anybody. I'm waiting till Malcolm comes home. He says he can get out now if he wanted to, 'cause being that he went to prison so young, by this time they think he should have realized his mistakes. And also being so young, he says they usually let them off a little easier. But I told him he might as well stay in for the two years and finish it out, 'cause he'll be on parole, and I feel that parole is just like being in prison. The parole officer coming into your house and you reporting to them at least once a week.

And I know about parole from Terrence. A year before Terry was born, Terrence got into trouble. He had bought one of those humongous radios, and he lent it to a friend, who took it on the street. It got stolen. But the guy it was stolen from knew the guy who stole it and told Terrence. Terrence went out there with a gun. But that night there was a block party, so the cops were just stopping people, checking them out for drugs. I guess Terrence looked suspicious 'cause he was real mad, so they searched him. And they're not supposed to just stop and search people like that. But they did, and they confiscated his gun. And I don't know if he had drugs on him. Anyway, he told them a lie—that he found the·gun on some street. So he got arrested. He got five years' probation for carrying an illegal weapon and 'cause he wouldn't tell them about no people involved in drugs. And the cops beat him bad. When he came home his face was all scratched, with lumps all over it. He was black and blue. He tried to do something about them cops beating him, but ain't nothing come out of that. The police didn't do a thing about those cops.

So I'll just wait for Malcolm to get out. He'll be worth the wait, 'cause he's unique. He's his own person. I'm shocked that I met a different kind of person. Not 'cause he's in prison,

but 'cause his whole outlook on things is different. I never
met a person like him before. A person that's kinda like me
in a way. But then again, he's more than what I am. He's
more outgoing, and I like that. He was shy at first, but now
he talks me to death.

Only thing is, we did almost break up last week. My uncle
called and asked me how involved I was with Malcolm. So I
said, "I love him. We have a relationship." And my uncle
was like, "I hate to tell you this." The first thought that came
into my mind was Malcolm's dead. Or he's in the hole. In
solitary. So he said, "Malcolm's a complete fuck-up. I want
you to leave him alone. Don't come here. And watch out for
him, 'cause he's gonna call you tonight." I was like, I'm gonna
leave him. My uncle was saying things like, "He's usin' you.
He wants you to bring him packages. He just wants a girl he
can sit down with and whatnot." So I'm sittin' there crying
and all upset.

Then Malcolm called about nine or ten. "Leticia," he said,
"your uncle told me that you're not coming up here no more.
That you're not gonna talk to me. That you're gonna cut me
off. So I just want to know. I don't want to lose no sleep over
this." And I was like, "Lose sleep? I thought you cared about
me." But he just told me to think about it and that he would
call me the next morning. And he did. And he told me what
happened between him and my uncle. It had to do with marijuana. Somehow they get it in there. I didn't bring him any
in. They can forget that! Leticia ain't bringing in no drugs.
But Malcolm had some, and he was supposed to give my
uncle some and he didn't. I couldn't believe it! "You mean to
tell me you're arguing over some doggone drugs?" I said to
Malcolm. "Come on, y'all should be beyond that. You're in
there for attempted murder, and you're arguing over some
petty drugs!" I had to laugh. I mean people get killed over a
penny. People fight over the littlest things. So Malcolm asked

me if I was gonna leave him. And I said, "No. I'm not." But ever since our discussion, I don't think that I'm gonna be as nice as I was. Coming up three times a week. I want him to think about this. I want him to call me and tell me how much he misses me.

JANUARY 21    I'm kind of exhausted now. I had a rough day. They brought a big delivery into the store, and we had to stock it all. And it's heavy boxes. Plus I do a little of everything there now. Deliveries, stacking. I even work the grill sometimes.

But I still love it, 'cause it's money. More money to help take care of my kids. Pay my bills. I have money in my pocket. And that's kind of hard to do by myself. Just getting a check from public assistance, after you pay the bills there ain't nothing left. With the job and my public assistance for the kids, I have money left over.

But now public assistance only gives me $208. And that's just for the kids. They cut me personally off, but I don't know why yet. It's not 'cause I'm making too much on my job. I bring home like $175 a week—$190 before taxes—and you can earn up to $5,000 a year, which I don't. So they cut my cash flow from $248.50 to $208. And I was getting $170 in food stamps, and now I'm getting $125. The only thing I know is I got a letter in the mail. It said as of January 1988, the cash flow would be decreased and food stamps would be decreased. For a family of three I was supposed to get $286 cash flow and $158 in food stamps. But they decreased both, and I don't understand why. I'll never understand how people can say public assistance makes people not want to work. Maybe there are some girls who sit around waiting for their checks. Who don't make an effort to try to get a job. And maybe people do take assistance until they're able to work. But it's a help until you can go out and get a job.

And there *are* certain circumstances that prevent you from

working at a certain time. Look at me. I had my kids. I don't have my high school diploma. And I do need to maintain my living arrangement. So I need public assistance until I'm able to go out and work and support myself completely. But I don't know how people can just live on welfare. They have to be getting money in somehow. They're doing something illegal or something, 'cause it's just not enough.

Then, too, if people go off public assistance and look for a job, they could lose their medical coverage. Like, now that I'm off, I'd have to pay something if me or my kids got sick, 'cause I don't get no work benefits. I couldn't afford that.

And the thing is, Terrence owes nine thousand dollars in back child support. The Bureau of Child Support said they were going to garnish his wages. But that remains to be seen. Nothing's happened so far. And I know that Terrence don't give me no money 'cause he thinks I'll go spend it on drugs. But I've changed. And he won't recognize that. But he does buy clothes and toys for Terry. He does help in that way.

You know, though, sometimes I think people in the welfare hotels have the right idea. They probably get fifteen thousand dollars a year, because they have to pay that rent, which is like a thousand dollars a month. And they probably get money for food and clothes and for pocket money. Anyway, that's the way it seems to me.

Truth is, though, that I would never want to live in those hotels. I mean when I was younger and I had nowhere to go. I vowed I'd never in my life . . . I'd rather sleep on a park bench than move into a welfare hotel. Or I'd build me a hut somewhere. Get some straw. Like one time me and my friend was walking over to Gracie Mansion, where Mayor Koch lives. It was summertime. And we walked into this little house made out of cardboard. And I said if I ever had a choice of a shelter or a hotel or living in the street, I'd do the same thing. I'd build me a cardboard house. And I'd have to survive.

———

I don't know, so much happens to me in one day. Like this week, the day before yesterday, I met this new guy at work. He called me after I got off work and came over that evening. And I was talking to him and everything, and he wants to get serious. Start dating. He's twenty-six years old and he's divorced, with a child. His name is Lorenzo. He just got out of the Marines a year ago. And he's going to Apex for mechanics. He works some nights. He's got his high school diploma. And he's very smart.

And you know, I do like him. He's intelligent. And he has good conversation. But I don't know him that well. I just met him two days ago. But he wants to date me. How can I do that, though! I'm with Malcolm. But I feel ashamed to tell him that Malcolm's in prison. It's like kind of hiding it. Hiding the relationship. And the way I feel is, to tell another man about this . . . it would make him feel so degraded. Here is one man in prison, and he's a bad dude. And here's another man busting his butt, trying to do good for hisself. And this woman's gonna say that she's seeing this guy in prison doing nothing for hisself or for her. She's still going to him. The good guy's gonna say, "Why you go with him? I mean he really can't do much for you, 'cause he's behind bars. Whereas *I* can, 'cause I'm out here." So I haven't told Lorenzo. Especially 'cause I met Malcolm in prison. It's not like I known him before he was sent there.

And then Malcolm, regardless of where he's at, it's him, the person, I like. OK, I say he made a mistake or two. I'm not happy about it. I'm not gonna praise him for it. But he's a person. And he's paying for his mistakes. And you know, Malcolm don't look like he could hurt a butterfly. Though you never know.

But Lorenzo, he's so kind. So sweet. I just don't know what to do, 'cause I don't want to hurt him either. I think about his feelings.

Then, too, with Malcolm, sometimes I'm really getting to

the point that I'm ready to give up visiting. It's like the feeling is dying down 'cause the relationship happened so fast. But then all my relationships start like that. My relationship to Terrence too. Like with all the others, I get tired of the person. I don't want to see him no more. And I'm tired of running up there. I see him every weekend now, and I want money in my pocket. And he ain't sent me none lately. All that money visiting him adds up.

———

By the way, I invited Terrence over tonight. This is just like the soap opera! I guess my voice was so sexy, he just couldn't resist. So he said OK. I feel like "All My Children." Like Natalie. She's always trying to play on a man. To use him or get a man. I mean I'm not actually trying to use a man. It's just that they come to me. I have so many. I have too many. And that's why I let them all go. But they won't go, you know. They're like dogs. When you have a puppy, he always stays with you. You can lose him, and he comes back.

But then, I'm the one who invited Terrence. I wanted to talk. It wasn't nothing really important at all. But I did tell him we need to start communicating more. There's a lot of things I want to tell him. How I feel about the situation we're in. 'Cause once we shared something very great. And now it's like we don't have nothing to say to each other. That's not right. Not right for Terry neither.

Sometimes I think about my relationships to men. I don't really know why they start up so fast. It's like when I meet a guy and he's interested and I am, I want to know more about him. I get involved with that person. And the next thing, it happens too fast. I can't understand that. It's like I know the whole person's life. His whole history. I know about his parents, everything, all in one day, 'cause I have questions. I'm curious.

And I see these guys as husbands in a way. I don't go out looking for no husband. But I do wonder what it's like to be married. I know what it's like to live with a man. And I sometimes wonder do I really want to do that again? I don't think so. I live with my brother, and he gets on my nerves. He asks me did I cook dinner. And I tell him, "What's wrong with you? You can't get in there and cook your own?" Then he asks me to get things for him. He just lays there in the bed, till I say, "Get up!" I'm not waiting on nobody. I mean I don't mind once in a while. But that's it.

When I think about an ideal marriage between me and a guy, it's about trust and communication. Trust and conversation. As long as you keep the conversation flowing and have trust in a man . . . 'Cause I really don't have that in any man. I mean he has to prove to me I can depend on him. He has to prove to me he's loyal and he's not physically abusive. I don't want that at all. But so far that's been cool in my relationships that I've had besides Terrence.

Still, I never can stay with a man too long. It's like moving all the time. I move a lot. From area to area. And when I move, I meet new guys wherever I go. And, too, it's just that I'm not satisfied. I remember this one guy when I was on crack. I was eighteen and he was a year older. We'd get high together. He was so in love with me. He'd never let me out of his sight. And that bothered me. I didn't like it. I was trying to make money, doing what I was doing . . . tricking. And one time I had this client at my house. In my bedroom. And we decided to make this other guy jealous. So when he knocked on the apartment door, I didn't answer. And he knew I was in there, 'cause I had the light on. So he went downstairs and he noticed the light was off. And when he came back up, he noticed it was on. So he started banging and kicking, calling my name from downstairs. Then he cried, "Leticia, I love you! How can you leave me?" Oh, God, I couldn't take it. Finally he stopped coming around. And now I regret it, 'cause he was so nice.

I know that men play into my having nice things. 'Cause now like Lorenzo's gonna get me my cable. And I just met him. He wants me so much that he's gonna do this. That s the good thing about having a man. And you know, I don't even ask them for nothing, neither. So maybe they do it 'cause I'm a nice person. Or maybe 'cause they feel I want them. Yes. Maybe that's it. 'Cause when I see a guy that looks good on the street—not only the way a person's face looks; I mean their appearance and everything—I say I *want* him. And I can kinda generally read people. I figure what they're about. So if I see a guy, I say, Well, maybe I should take a chance. Then I go for it. And I get what I want.

But I don't see myself as sexy. I'm plain. A guy told me that once. I'm an ordinary girl. Just an everyday person. I do pay attention to the way I look, though. Like I went today and bought this outfit. And I'm going to tease the hell out of Malcolm with it. Just to satisfy myself, I'm gonna really tease him. And it's real nice. A white miniskirt and tight white top.

But I'll tease him in a very subtle way. I'm not gonna jump all over him. Put it like that: I will be noticeable! And I already put my hair in these cornrows and dyed it blond. I'll wear a hairpiece woven into the braids, and I'll look *real* nice. And I'll just ask Malcolm, "Why are you attracted to me?" And he's gonna say, "Look how you dress."

But I'm also outspoken. And I think guys like that too. I'm a person who speaks my mind. I don't have to put on a front for any man. Most women do, you know. They have to try to impress guys. Not me. I don't try to impress any man. They have to accept me for what I am.

Right now, though, I'm so mad at Malcolm. He's in the box right now. Solitary confinement. He did something very stupid. His big mouth. When they called him to get in lineup, they told everybody to be quiet. So he had to open his mouth to tell the others to be quiet. Then they wrote him up a ticket. The last time he was in solitary it was for twelve days, and they told him if he got any more tickets within six months that he'd get solitary for fifteen days. So he got a ticket. And he got this ticket when he was already in solitary! And now he just got another one for the same thing. And every ticket's for according to what you did. The last one he got was for fighting and putting a dude in the hospital. And I don't know, he's supposed to come out this Monday. But he may have to do more days. But he still gets visits and everything on the weekend. And he can go into the yard. He just can't get no packages. No food. And he's in a box room, under lock and key.

But he told me this last Saturday. "Leticia," he said, "I know what my problem is. I got a big mouth." 'Cause he is outspoken. And he does it at the wrong times. That's what gets him into trouble. So I told him, "Malcolm, why can't you just be quiet? When someone is talking, just don't say nothing." But sometimes, you know, I kinda figure he doesn't want to get out of prison. Maybe he just wants to stay there. Well, good luck. Good riddance to him. Because I got Lorenzo.

So Saturday, when I see Malcolm, I'm gonna lose him. I can let him down easy. I'm gonna tell him I'm not gonna come back up here no more. And I'm not gonna come visit him. I'm not gonna bring him no packages. All this is gone. And I'm gonna dress in my tight white outfit 'cause I want to see him get mad. When he puts me through these things I want to see him suffer. That's my satisfaction. Having me comin' up there all the time. I'm gonna get even.

Then, too, when I see him, I'm gonna ask him, "Why are you so stupid?" Me and his sister had a long talk. She says he's got an attitude problem. It's true. He thinks everything's supposed to go his way. That he's the boss of everything. It don't work that way. When he comes home, you got rules and laws and regulations you have to follow. The world does not revolve around Malcolm.

One thing, though, I learned. 'Cause all my relationships got some kind of teaching. And all of them seems so similar.

What's the same is, I leave all the guys. They all satisfy me sexually. Except for two or three. But I guess I left the rest 'cause they just didn't satisfy me *personally*. It don't have nothing to do with intercourse. It's just about pleasing me. I guess I want a man to bow down to me. I want a man to do what I want all the time. Once in a while he could be aggressive on his own part, but I'd rather he'd bow down to me. I'd rather control him. Be the boss.

It's like what I tell Terry now. I say, "I want to raise you to be a man that I would want to marry. Kindhearted. Understanding. Someone who would sympathize." Maybe, like, it'd be that time of month where I would need time to myself. And he'd understand. Be loving about it. "OK, honey, fine. I can understand how you feel right now." That kinda thing would be an expression of sympathy. He'd be able to compromise. Not get everything he wants.

But I'm weird. I want a whole lot in a little bit of time. And Malcolm's like that too. I want my way, and he wants his way. And I think that's why we don't get along. So I don't see a relationship going on a long time right now. Like I was thinking the other day, I said to myself, Leticia, will you be married? Can you ever stay with a man a long period of time? Besides the four years I was with Terrence? I don't know. I can't say.

I don't know if I'm gonna tell Malcolm about ending our relationship this weekend or not. I don't want to hurt his feelings. But then again, he's so stubborn it might not even affect him. Then I think, If he cared anything about me, or enough about me, he wouldn't let me leave him. So I'm not sure what I'll do.

**JANUARY 26**    *Leticia over the telephone*
I won't be able to make my appointment today, 'cause I have to be home early for my grandmother. And oh, by the way, I just wanted to tell you I'm getting married! I'm marrying

Malcolm and moving to Newburgh, New York, in April, after the wedding. That's where he wants to live. He proposed to me on Saturday, and I realized I loved him. That I want to be with him even though I'll have to wait till 1990.

**FEBRUARY 11**    *I phoned Leticia at work because she didn't show up at my house as scheduled. Told she was ill, I called her at home. When she answered, she sounded groggy and her words were slurred. She was disoriented.*

**LETICIA:** Checkers Restaur . . .

**J. SANDER:** Is something the matter? You sound sick.

**LETICIA:** No. I'm not sick. I'm having personal problems. I'm on crack.

*I asked Leticia to put her grandmother on the phone, but first she put Terry on instead.*

**MRS. WILSON**    Leticia has been out all night and left the children with her brother. When I arrived at her apartment this morning, Leticia came home soon after. She was crying and very upset. She told me she was with a girl who had a seizure. I called Leticia's social worker at the Y, whom Leticia hasn't seen in a long time. But I don't really know what to do. I feel Leticia is exhausting herself by working all week and staying out on weekends and during the week as well. I feel like Leticia is a lot like my father. He was an alcoholic and has been at death's doorstep many times. They swear they're not going to try those drugs again, and then they do. I don't know what I can do about it. She can pick up that stuff anywhere she wants to around here.

**FEBRUARY 12 AND 14**    *I called Leticia, but she was out both times. Mrs. Wilson told me Leticia seemed better. She hadn't been taking any drugs that she knew of.*

**FEBRUARY 17**    *Phone conversation with Leticia*

**LETICIA:** I'm better now. Everything's fine. I'm not working at Checkers anymore. I'm gonna stay home and help my grandmother take care of the children she takes in. She's going to pay me. This way I won't be running all over the place. I'll call you in the next couple of weeks when things straighten out.

J. SANDER: What about the drug situation? Have you taken any more crack?

LETICIA: No. I'm not gonna do that.

MARCH 4    *I met with Leticia in her apartment. Her grandmother was there, along with six children ranging in age from a few months to two years old. Leticia sat at a kitchen table, talking to me in a monotone, showing me pictures of Hazela's first birthday, Leticia's twenty-first birthday, and the Thanksgiving ceremony at the Y she had asked me to attend with her. She also showed me a photograph of a baby she had cut out of* Ebony *magazine, and asked me rather longingly if I didn't think this was a pretty baby. We exchanged some remarks about how young Hazela was and how cuddly she was, even though she was now walking. Leticia told me she was very tired and discouraged. Then she said, "I just found out I failed my GED. I tried to better myself. But I can't. So I'm not gonna do anything more."*

*Mrs. Wilson tried to encourage her, letting her know that a lot of people have disappointments but that she had to go on. But Leticia was visibly distressed about failing the exam. "It was my last chance to get ahead," she said.*

*That was my last meeting with Leticia. She refused contact with me until August 1990.*

# PART III

## Can
## Anyone
## Help?

# 12 ■ *"Every time the phone rings, my heart stops in my mouth"*

## Rena Wilson

**MARCH 7, 1988**    I could see Leticia was going downhill. She used to do the dishes and the laundry. But ever since she failed her GED, she's done neither. She comes in and goes to sleep. "Everything is so overwhelming, Gramma," she said. "I can't make any money on my job. I have to take Hazela and Terry for appointments, and I can't miss my work. It's too much. I can't take this kind of responsibility."

Leticia told me she was very angry about failing her test, and I could understand that. But I have been working hard myself, trying to put money into the apartment, and I need her help. She could quit her job if it's too hard. I said I would give her one hundred dollars a week to help me care for the children I take in. And she had a three-hundred-dollar phone bill to that prisoner. She suggested that some of the money she could earn would be put toward that. But if Leticia wants to stay in her state of euphoria again, there's little I can do. We all have our fears of failing. We have to go on and do our work anyway.

Leticia has been talking about having Terry go back to his father. She had a purpose to get over crack the first time, because she wanted Terry with her. But now she thinks maybe she can't handle him anyway. That he should go live with his father again. But I don't want Terry to go back to that family. They tend to overindulge the child.

At this point I don't really know what to do. I'm just so scared Hazela will go into a foster home, and I just couldn't do that. We're all going to have to work this out. I'm going to call Leticia's mother, though I'm afraid of Hazela going to stay at their house with that stepfather there. I don't want anything to go on with him. All I know is if worse comes to worse, I'll have to take in two less children. With Hazela and Terry, that would be seven kids, and that's too much for me. I will call my mother too. I can't have those children separated.

MARCH 21    Leticia's still with it. Still on that crack. She was supposed to go to her counselor at the Y today to be admitted to New York Hospital for a ten-day detox program and then to long-term treatment. She went down to the hospital with her mother. But as soon as they arrived, Leticia decided that she didn't need help. She just walked out of the hospital. And several days before that, her mother had taken her to Beth Israel Hospital. But you need a letter of referral there, and Leticia hadn't brought one. She hadn't bothered.

Leticia is just not responsible now, so I've had to start staying in the apartment the last two weeks. One morning I came here and she was just getting home from her nighttime activities. She had left the two kids completely alone. She's very erratic.

And I know she's been very tired lately from running to that crack house. She says she's going to visit her friends, but I know otherwise. She's out to get that stuff. She comes home every few days, hungry and exhausted. She'll play with

Hazela for a few minutes, but she seems very lackadaisical. Without spirit. And she's stopped worrying about Hazela's food, though she probably knows I'll take care of it.

Terry is going to stay with his father for the weekend. Leticia told me maybe I should tell Terrence to keep the child another few weeks, but I don't want them getting wind of this drug stuff. Besides, Leticia's other grandmother, Doreen, said she would help me care for the other six children sometimes. If it turns out she can't, I will tell some of the mothers I just won't be able to take care of their kids. I don't want to do this. But sometimes you have to do things and hope the rest straightens out.

MARCH 29    I'm going to court tomorrow to plead my case for temporary kinship foster care of the children. If you're a member of the family and another member can't any longer deal with a child, you're allowed to become a foster parent. It will be a great relief to me. I don't know what else to do, since Leticia's away for several days at a time now. Last Monday she called to see if she could visit Hazela. She was incoherent, so I told her no. I was afraid that she would take Hazela away. In fact, I called the police to ask them what my rights are. And they told me if she sounds at all rational, she could take the kids with her legally. I wouldn't have a leg to stand on. Like last week Leticia took Hazela to Leticia's father's house over my objections. She told me that she wanted to stay there. But she came back quickly, saying that her father wasn't going to let her live there without paying some money. Then she told me she gave him her food stamps. But now I can't tell when Leticia's lying. It's very possible that she sold them to other people in order to get money for crack. Of course, if I were to say that to her, she'd only get angry. "You don't understand what I'm all about," she says. "You never believe anything I say."

———

We gave Leticia an ultimatum. Me, her mother, the worker from the Bureau of Child Welfare. If she didn't go into a rehab program, I would become the permanent foster mother. But Leticia doesn't understand what's happening. She constantly wants to know why I'm doing this. "If they're my children," she says, "why are people taking them away? People use alcohol and other drugs, and I can walk away from this anytime I want." But the children have to be protected. She's using the stuff pretty heavily now. My neighbors have told me that she's been asking them for small amounts of money here and there. And I think one of the reasons she didn't go into a rehab in the first place was that she wanted to go down and get her welfare check. That way, she'd have more money for drugs. If she only had gone into a program, I wouldn't have to be doing this.

I don't even know where she's living now. I found out that she spent one night in an apartment upstairs. But those people are also on crack. And Vernon has told me that one night he and his sister had met some guys dabbling in the stuff. When he told her not to take it, she said, "Mind your own business!"

The truth is, I can't trust Leticia any longer. I feel there's a possibility of real danger when she comes home on crack. The other day she put a TV dinner in the stove and completely forgot about it. So now I'm afraid of fires. And what if she tries to hurt me? I'm scared of crack. You hear so many stories these days. I don't know if she'd physically harm me or the children. And what if she gets involved in some kind of criminal element, the way she did before?

I have to tell you, sometimes I wonder if Leticia has a flaw in her general makeup. If this isn't genetic in some way. Is she like her father's side of the family? Almost that whole side seems to be of weak character. A lot of them take drugs. They succumb to the easiest thing for them.

Leticia seems past knowing what the truth is anymore.

The way I feel is, taking crack is just another way of committing suicide. But sometimes I wonder, did her childhood cause this?

APRIL 4    I am going to have a hearing in June to get permanent foster care of Hazela. Leticia didn't listen to our ultimatum. She's still out on drugs. In the meantime, the worker from the Bureau of Child Welfare did give me temporary orders. Now at least Leticia won't be able to take Hazela away, although I don't think she's even up to doing that at this point. The other day, when Leticia came to the door, she was quite tearful. I told her that Hazela was sleeping, and she just said, "Oh, that's all right. I'll go away and come back another time." I think she's scared to see Hazela. But I said, "No, you can come in. It's time to wake her up." When Hazela got up, she recognized Leticia and kept saying, "Mama." But Leticia only asked if she could have some of her clothes. She wanted to change here. I didn't want her to think that she could stay here anytime she wanted to, because the stipulations of being a foster parent say if the real mother stays in the same house, the foster mother risks losing the child. So I told her she could get her clothes, have something to eat and drink, but then she'd have to leave. When I asked her if she needed any help or if she wanted to talk to anybody about rehabilitation, she said no.

It's curious. Before today I had noticed she came by looking very raggedy. All of her clothes were messy. Now it seems she wants to keep herself looking nice. She asked for all of her hair stuff. Why? When she left, I told her that I hope everything goes OK. But Leticia looks forlorn. She cries at the slightest drop of a hat. You can tell she isn't herself. That she has been through a lot. I can see that she's thinking about what she's done. What she's given up. You can tell from her sadness. She acts very humble to me.

———

I feel good about getting temporary custody of Hazela. I mean for her sake. I know I can take good care of her. But I did tell the BCW worker that if Leticia does get herself together, I would have no trouble giving her back her child. I'm a mother myself, and although I don't know what it would be like to lose a child, I can imagine from when I was forced to put my child in that foundling home.

The truth is, I feel worse about Terry. He's been staying with Terrence at Terrence's parents' house. I can't really take care of both of them right now, with Terry having to go to school in the morning and the other kids coming here early. Doreen wasn't able to help me with the children, as it turned out, because her daughter is also on drugs, so she has to mind her grandchildren too. But the thing was that I saw Terry and Terrence's family in court at the foster care hearing. Terry acted like he didn't even know me. He turned his head away. When I approached him and said, "What are you doing? How come you're acting like you don't know Gramma?" he smiled and looked the other way. And he's begun calling Terrence's mother "Mommy." I'm afraid the family is telling him to do that. So I simply told Terrence to remember that Terry had a sister. That it would be nice if they saw each other from time to time. But I'm scared they won't let me see Terry.

It's all very complicated now. We were friends before Leticia had her custody fight with them. At that time, they swore at me when I wanted her to take him back, and they threatened to break my arms. They were real nasty. I can't in good conscience be civil to that family now.

And, too, the way I feel, Terrence had not come through with any real child support when Leticia was caring for Terry on her own. When she was off of drugs the first time. He owed her a lot of money for the child. And it was supposed to be taken from his wages, but it never was. And I know he'll get custody this time, and it really bothers me. The bureaucracy doesn't care about *who's* taking care of the child, or especially *how* the child is taken care of. And that's even true with abused children. If you try to get help, you're given the complete runaround.

And I know this from Leticia's case itself. Nobody did anything when they were told she was being abused. When I finally found out, I called the child-abuse hot line, and the authorities did nothing. The way I feel is people try to get something done and they can't accomplish it, so they give up. Sometimes I wonder if that's why Leticia feels that nothing good can really happen with her now. Because the old things were allowed to go for so long.

Even with the drug situation as bad as it is today, you call the twenty-four-hour hot line and often they don't answer. And if they do, nothing much happens. When I called them this time when I knew Leticia was on drugs, they didn't come and pick her up and they didn't tell me what I should do. The city and the laws, they essentially promise you the world and give you nothing.

APRIL 14    Every time the phone rings, my heart stops in my mouth. I think they're going to tell me something's happened to Leticia. That she's had her arms broken again. She's been stabbed. That she's dead. I know it's hard for both of us at this point, but maybe it's even harder for me. I'm taking care of six children from seven-thirty in the morning to seven o'clock at night.

But worst of all, I am totally confused about her. I talked to a drug analyst down at the hearing, and he told me, "Don't mention rehabilitation. When you see her, just ask her how she is. And don't give her any money." But all this is very difficult when you care about someone. When you have tried to be there for that person.

I know I go back and forth. Like the other night, Leticia came by to get her mail. She said she would be back again a few

days later, to see Hazela. I was relieved to see her, but then
again I wasn't, because she's in and out, in and out. So I
decided I'm not going to let her coming and going bother me
anymore. I've made up my mind that I have to go on with
the process of living. I've gone about as far as I can go with
these drugs. Next week I'm going to box up her clothes. I
need the closet space here.

In fact, right now I'm leaning toward making this apartment my home. I'm paying two rents, which I can't afford. I've been living with my other daughter, Leticia's aunt,
and though she and her husband say it is OK that I take
Hazela there, there's a lot of commotion with a baby. And
if Terry comes back, I'll need a home for both of them.
Then, too, there are the children I take in. I need the space
now.

APRIL 22    Yesterday Leticia came by for her Medicaid card.
She comes at the times I'm most busy, wanting to see Hazela.
This time she said she needed aspirin and Vaseline. But she
gave no reasons why. She has lost a lot of weight and looks
terrible. There's a vacant stare to her now, though every time
she sees Hazela her eyes fill up like she wants to cry. When
I suggested I would send some more of her clothes over, she
said, "I don't have any residence at the moment." So I told
her, "Well, that's too bad. You did have a place here." She
said, "I know, Gramma." She's very docile. I think it's the
crack.

She looks like she could use some hospitalization to get
the drugs out of her system. What can I do? I'm assuming
this is what she herself wants. She wants to leave here. But I
think she's more or less living from hand to mouth now. It
distresses me so.

I tell you, I'm not really angry at Leticia, though I do think
she has had it better than a lot of people. She has had help.
I would say I do feel very disappointed. If she can't cope with
things, I just can't understand that. She had so much going
for her. She is so smart. She's a person with talents too.

**MAY 10**    I attach a lot of importance to a mother's love. So sometimes when I think about Leticia I get very upset. I think about her childhood. This whole thing is so distorted. My own daughter, her mother—I can't understand how she could continue to live with a man who molested her daughter. I know her mother finds it hard to make decisions, so maybe that was it. She couldn't tell him to leave. I never did understand. After she first married this man, a lot of times she would call me and say, "Mom, can you let me have five dollars? I don't have any food for the kids." And I would give her twenty-five dollars or thirty dollars, because what was she going to do with five? And often I would go running down there to help her. The refrigerator was bare, and she would get into these depressive states and start crying. And I would wonder what on earth was going on.

Then, too, I know for a fact that for a long time her husband wasn't working. And she was just barely working herself. So whenever Leticia and Vernon would come up to me, whenever they allowed the children to come to me, I would give them food to take home. But they would always say to each other, "I'm gonna take my food into my room and eat it, and you're not going to get any of *my* food." And if I would give them money, they would tell me, "Gramma, I'm gonna spend this money before I get home, because they'll just take it from us."

I never knew what was going on. Although one time, I do remember, I'd been to their apartment and I noticed that . . . you know how you see something but your mind tells you no, this is not happening. But one time I was down there and Leticia was sitting on her stepfather's lap. She was about nine or ten years old. And he had his hand draped on her in a funny way, and she had her arm about him. It seemed peculiar to me, the way they were acting with each other. Too close. But then I thought I might have been feeling that way because I don't ever remember sitting on my father's lap. Just maybe when I was real young. So I cast it off.

It was only later, when Leticia started running away to be with Terrence, that I just kept thinking and thinking about the whole situation. What was the matter with this child? I'm a deep thinker, and if I have something to turn around in my mind, I may not think it all out at one time. But when I have the opportunity to really sit down, I do give it time.

Like at one point, when Leticia was about fourteen years old, she confided in her aunt that she was having sex with Terrence. We were all very upset about this because she was so young. When my daughter Enid told me, I remember I sat down with Leticia and we talked about sex and babies. And then this thought came into my mind, and I asked her, "Is anything going on at home that you'd like to talk to me about?" And she said no. So I came out and said it: "Does your stepfather ever molest you?" She just looked at me and she didn't say anything. And I said to her, "Well, you really don't have to answer me if you would rather not, but I'm going to ask you again. If you don't want to tell me, just say, 'Gramma, I'd rather not answer.' " But when I asked her that time, she said, "Yes. He has molested me." And I said, "Well, how long was this going on?" And she said, "Since I was five."

I was in a state of shock! I didn't know what to do. It was then, after I spoke to my daughter Enid, that we decided to call BCW. But even when I reported it to them and went down to confront Denise with it, she seemed to feel Leticia was lying. She said she felt Leticia wanted to hit the streets and be out with Terrence, and she was making up this excuse to get what she wanted. I just can't see people living in a house in close proximity and you don't know what's going on.

At some point the BCW worker did finally see all of us: Leticia, me, and Denise. But they never saw the stepfather. And they told me he was going to be prosecuted. But even while Leticia continued to run away, they never did prosecute him.

Finally Leticia and I did sit down and talk about her living somewhere else. So she went to live with Enid and her husband and daughter. Unfortunately, though, things didn't work out there either. She didn't follow their rules. One night when she didn't come home there, I went to find her at Terrence's. I saw Leticia and Terrence coming out of his sister's apartment. I said to him that I wanted to meet his sister, and I went up there. It was atrocious. Very dark. You couldn't see anything. There were three or four boys just sitting there in chairs, sleeping. So I knew this was no situation for her to be in. My daughter wouldn't take her back by that point, so I did. But my husband gave me a lot of static, and finally he put her out. That's finally how she came to live with Terrence. I tell you, I spent very trying times over this whole thing.

Now, when I've asked Denise to help with Hazela, I have specifically told her that I do not want Hazela taken to her house. And on two occasions she has taken her there anyway. So now, if I go out on a weekend, I get a baby-sitter. And I think my daughter understands what I'm saying, because she tells me, "Oh, well, Mama, I'll keep the baby with me. I'll never leave her alone. I'll watch her at all times." But I'll tell her if she can't watch Hazela here, she won't be of any service to me. But how can she herself stay with that man? I just don't know.

JUNE 12    I petitioned for custody of Terry a couple of weeks ago, but the court date was postponed until August 4. I'm following my better judgment to try to get him. I want the family to stay together. Terry shouldn't be separated from his sister. Both my legal counsel and the BCW worker discouraged me about getting custody of him, but I know I would always think about Terry and his going to that family if I didn't try. Nothing beats a failure but a failure to try.

AUGUST 4    I was at Family Court. Waited there all day, until seven at night. I told Leticia about the hearing, and she came at eleven o'clock. Terrence and his parents got to court a bit later. Leticia's counselor from the Y was also there, trying to talk to her. But Leticia can't understand. All she says is, "Why is everyone butting in? I'm twenty-one years old." But she looked terrible. She's pencil thin. She's lost a great deal of weight. She's down to about one hundred and ten pounds, and she's five feet ten. She had fixed her hair nicely, though. I could see that.

Then, as if we're not having enough problems, Leticia told the judge that she's tried to visit Hazela and that I wouldn't let her, that I threw her out. She's putting the burden on me. Here I have been trying to help her. I tried to get her treatment. If she had gone into a rehab, I wouldn't have to be in court. I'm very angry about how she's treating me now. Her counselor keeps telling me, "Drugs are doing this. She's not responsible for what she says." But I don't agree.

By the time the hearing was over, I did get visitation rights for Hazela to see Terry on the weekend. Leticia can also see her children once a week at my home. But the judge didn't even question Leticia about drugs. She read that Leticia was taking PCP. The BCW worker had told the judge she had used it. But they couldn't produce the report verifying it, so it never came up.

When I told the judge that I was concerned about Leticia coming to my home, all the judge said was, "Well, take the children to BCW, and Leticia can visit them there." But that's extremely inconvenient. I have to wait until Terry is delivered to me, and Terrence never tells me what time he's coming. I've asked Terrence to call me a day ahead about his plans to bring Terry. But sometimes he doesn't do it. He'll just show up. Or sometimes he'll tell me when he's coming and then come hours later. I wait at home the whole day, for fear I'll miss him. So how will I know when I can go to BCW? How do I even reach Leticia to tell her? I told the judge I'll try to go along with it, but if I feel threatened by Leticia or if it is too difficult, I'm going to stop.

There's just something wrong with the whole system of child care in this city. No one looks at who's helping the child or how he's being taken care of. Look at Terry! I'm worried about him. They spoil the child. If he's going to grow up, he needs a semblance of order. Giving Terry everything he wants is not building character.

This city doesn't take care of its children. The way I see it, people just look at the law and they get rid of each case as fast as possible. Go right on to the next. The judge at the hearing asked a lot of fast questions. A person just feels intimidated. But the children suffer, and people who would take good care of a child don't have the chance because there's so much trouble getting custody to help out.

And what is the city doing about drugs? About children and drugs? Crack is everywhere. Innocent people aren't safe. Pushers take advantage of young children. Ten- and eleven-year-olds are used to deliver the goods. And the authorities? What do they do? They don't save the children.

AUGUST 25    You know, I've always been someone who sympathizes with the next person. But I've changed. I don't sympathize with Leticia, because she's gone to the enemy. My main goal now is to give Hazela a chance in life. I couldn't let her go with Leticia. It would've been another life lost. I couldn't stand by and see her go the way her mother has. You know, it's one thing to give a child a home; it's another thing to take care of a child. Maybe Leticia could give her a place to live. But that's it.

Hazela gives me strength to go on. She's delightful. She's very jealous of me being with the other children and doesn't want to share me with them. She wants me to pick her up constantly. It's "Gamma" early in the morning, 5:30 A.M. I struggle to the kitchen to get her bottle. She's my welcoming committee! I rest knowing I'm doing what I'm obligated to do. But I can't congratulate myself, because I'm a washed-out rag at the end of the day.

**SEPTEMBER 3**    Leticia has made it a point to tell me, "I'm living around the corner." On 129th Street they have a lot of abandoned buildings. There's an influx of a certain kind of people. I don't like to put people in categories, because people are the way they are for some reason, but I know many of them are on crack. And Leticia tells me, "Gramma, you would be surprised at the number of people taking crack where I am and in your apartment building too."

**SEPTEMBER 10**    Hazela is fighting a lot with the other children, and she runs around like a rabbit. She has real energy. Runs headlong into things, while I have my heart in my mouth. I just hope her energy will be put into something useful later on. But still, she's doing well. And I'm pleased I'm taking care of her. I just couldn't have put her into a foster home. I suppose my family wouldn't have let that happen, but my mother is up in age and my daughters have their own families. So I just pray my health stays good.

Leticia still comes by from time to time to visit her. Hazela knows her and calls her Mommy. I can see Leticia gets sad when she sees her, though, and she doesn't stay long. Terry gets very upset when he comes to visit and Leticia is here. He will say, "Mommy, I love you." Then, when Leticia leaves, he gets stomachaches. I know it's taking a toll on him.

**SEPTEMBER 28**    Leticia was here for a few days, even though I'm not supposed to let her stay legally. But she said she wanted to go to Beth Israel Hospital for detoxification, so I thought it would be better if she stayed here until we went. We had gone there again this past Saturday, and they said they did have a bed for her. But now she has no Medicaid card. And that's a huge problem. The city cut her off Medicaid like they cut her off welfare. It seems from what Leticia said that welfare found out about her drugs because they had put her into a work program and then realized on the job that she was using the stuff. They referred her to Metropolitan Hospital for treatment. But when they found out that she never went and that she quit the job, they took away her public assistance. They did give her an extension of a month for her food stamps and for Medicaid. And they told her that she could ask for a hearing prior to her cutoff day. But she didn't follow through with any of it. She never went to court.

She and I did go to the Medicaid office, though, to get an emergency card. But she couldn't get that because she had to have certain documents. She needed proof of where she lives. A rent receipt, a telephone bill. The problem is, she doesn't have an address. I can't let her use mine because I could lose Hazela. So we put down she was staying with my mother. But they checked with her, and she didn't want to sign anything. She's scared of this whole drug business. Leticia's mother couldn't provide an address because she lives in a project and she'd have to get a letter of permission from management before she could have anyone else in her home officially.

The people at the Medicaid office did give us a temporary card, however, and the woman there told us, "If Leticia goes into the hospital she will be able to use this. Just have the doctor fill it out and send it back to us. We will pay the bill."

The woman told us to be at the hospital at 7:00 A.M. sharp. So we left home at 5:45. When we got there, we found out the clinic didn't open until 9:00. We walked around and had breakfast, and when we went back they told us that they did have one bed for a female. But then when Leticia went downstairs to take care of the papers, the woman in charge there said she had to have more than a temporary Medicaid card and that she needed to have an address. But when we explained to her that Leticia couldn't get any documentation of address, she told her to go to a shelter. That she could use that as her address. So that's what we decided to do.

Meanwhile, though, Leticia was suffering with these pains in her stomach, so we went to the emergency room. But they wouldn't give her any medicine. "I'm sorry," the woman said. "We can't do this unless she pays." And I didn't have enough money with me. What made me mad, this episode was right after the doctor had told her she had a bad vaginal infection and gave her a prescription to be filled.

I was so distraught that I told the woman, "You know, you have a person who's trying to help herself, and I'm sure the medicine bill can be straightened out later." But she just said, "You don't have the right card. The other office made a mistake in giving it to you. You'll have to come back with the proper one."

When Leticia and I got home, her mother and I talked to her about going into a shelter. That it was the only way she could get into a program. Her mother knew about one shelter on Twenty-sixth Street. But Leticia just said, "No way! I won't go into one of those things."

A day later, though, she did change her mind. I told her I would go with her. So we went down there, but I couldn't stay with her long. The lady said that only the person that was applying could wait at that particular place. I could have waited downstairs, but it would have been two or three hours before all the papers were settled. Since my grandson was watching all the kids, I decided to go home.

An hour later, Leticia called. "Gramma, I don't think this shelter is going to be good for me, because I can't get a letter for the hospital before 7:00 A.M. tomorrow morning. When I called Beth Israel again, they said I had to be there before six tonight or they'd give up the bed." I asked her if she was sure she got the story straight. All she said was, "Yes, and I'm coming home."

I called the shelter myself. Finally I got through to the right person. The worker was very nice and told me she had said to Leticia that she would have to stay in the shelter twenty-four hours and that one is only allowed to leave after 7:00 A.M. But then she added to me, "You know, really we're not supposed to take her here with her drug condition. She belongs in another shelter. This shelter is for people who are able to work. We send them out on various jobs." But the worker said, "Since it's only a day, however, we will accept her and give her the letter she needs in time. Tell Leticia to come back."

I can't tell you how relieved I felt. When Leticia came home, I explained it all to her. But she wanted no part of the shelter. "Oh, Gramma," she said, "you should have seen those people. They were all dirty. The beds are side by side. Who knows if I'm laying there, maybe somebody would kill me. I would really be afraid to sleep there." Then, an hour later, some boyfriend of Leticia's stopped by and they went out to the movies. That was the end of the shelter.

But you know, in some ways I think she was not only upset about the shelter itself. She was afraid of what the woman had told her at Beth Israel about detoxification. And I was there when the woman said it, so I know she heard it right. Leticia had asked about the program. What they did there. And the lady said, "Well, all they do is just lock you in for seven or eight days and you walk up and down and look at television." I don't know if she was joking with Leticia. Sometimes people say things to make it seem easier, but I did ask if there was any counseling. All she said was, "If they need it." So Leticia reminded me of that when she got home from the shelter. She said, "Gramma, since that's what they do, I could do that here." I had to tell her that I thought she needed extensive counseling and that being locked up wasn't enough. But Leticia didn't listen.

I'll tell you, if Leticia really wants to get into a drug program, if there was anything I could do to help her, I'd be the first one, because she would be helping herself. But at this point

I feel very frustrated. The bureaucracy is putting up so many obstacles. I personally feel if someone is doing something detrimental to themselves and they seek help, they should be given it. And I know Leticia's scared to death. She called her counselor the other day and told her she was thinking of committing suicide.

But then I'm also upset with her. It's her own fault she doesn't have all these papers. That she doesn't have a Medicaid card and welfare and a place to live. All of these things being taken away, that's a part of what's happened to her with drugs. The other day she sat here and said, "I don't know how I ever got myself into all this. Letting my welfare go. My Medicaid." And I said to her, "I guess you're too much into crack. You just don't care." And she said, "Gramma, you're right." But then, even so, when a person is down like that, how do they get up?

OCTOBER 7    Leticia is becoming more and more desperate. The other day she said she was going to go to Harlem Hospital to see if she could apply for a Medicaid card there. Her counselor had set up this appointment. The woman at the hospital gave her a form to fill out and told her she needed a lease or a telephone bill for proof of address. Plus she had to report to the unemployment office. She had just been through all that! So Leticia went out on a binge. She got high. I didn't see her from Friday until the next Monday. That Monday when she came here, it was about five in the afternoon. She said, "Gramma, I'm not going to stay. I just have to make a very important phone call." She dialed 911 for the police. I heard her tell them that she had been sexually assaulted. She asked them to come over. "I can't give you the address of where I am," she said, "but I'll meet you in front of such and such a building right away." When she got off, she started screaming, "I hate men! I'm telling you that I hate them." Then she started procrastinating. I told her she had to go meet the police, but she said, "Oh, well, I'm not going to bother, 'cause what difference is it going to make?" But I could tell she had been using drugs. Even when she arrived, she couldn't sit down. She kept jumping up, and she was swaying back and forth. It was difficult to understand everything she was saying.

Then she asked me if she could change her clothes. "I'm going back out now," she said. And she left. I had no idea what to do. That night at three in the morning there was this loud bang on the door. Vernon asked who it was, and it was Leticia. When he told me she was back, I told him, "Just tell her to go away." But he couldn't do it, so he asked me to. I went to the door, and she was mumbling and crying. "My stomach is hurting me. My feet are all swollen up. I can't walk. Can't you let me in?" I told her, "No." And she said, "I have no place to go." And I told her, "Well, you have to go back to wherever you came from."

When she left, I looked outside from my terrace and saw her go over to one of the benches outside. She was crying. By that time I was totally unnerved. Vernon asked me why her feet were swollen. I didn't know. So he suggested that he go downstairs and take her a pair of my sneakers. I could hear her crying as he talked to her.

I was up the rest of the night, thinking about her. I said to myself, if she's really trying to get help, this is not helping her. In the morning she was still on the bench. I knew the security guards would come and make her move, so I went downstairs. "Leticia," I said, "come up. We'll try to call one more place and get you into a program." And she said, "Gramma, that's what I want to do. I can't control myself anymore." So we called another place, and they told us they had a long waiting list. That she should sign up but that it would take weeks, possibly months, before there would be a place for her. That night she was back on the street again.

What scares me now is how these drugs are affecting her brain, her thinking power. She has slurred speech all the time. Often she's totally incoherent. She told me she slept in the basement of a building for two months. And she's slept on park benches. Yet she's afraid to go to a shelter.

I guess, in the end, I'm one of these never-say-die people. I am a firm believer in where there's light, there's hope. Somewhere along the line, she may see the light. Who knows what might happen? All of a sudden she'll get the help she needs and turn herself around. I mean it can happen, you know.

**DECEMBER 2**     Well, I have very good news! Leticia did go into a program two weeks ago. She told me she realized she couldn't run from her past forever. She discussed her drugs with a friend of hers who is in AA, and he took her to a clinic in central Harlem. They transferred her with an escort to a place downtown. It seems like a very good place. I went to see it with Leticia's mother. And Leticia likes the facility a lot. They give them a five-dollar-a-week stipend, and they even take them to plays and out shopping. But they're always escorted. She said that through therapy, she's beginning to understand herself. She has to stay there for eighteen to twenty-four months. And the program offers a GED. She's even invited us to a Christmas celebration, and we're all going. In fact, Leticia's helping to organize it. Thank the Lord things will be all right!

**JANUARY 15, 1989**     Leticia was kicked out of the detox program. She was caught out of the building with a boy from her program. They're very strict about those things: leaving the premises without a chaperon. It's too bad. We all went there for the Christmas festivities, and it was so nice. Leticia looked much better. She had gained back a lot of weight. Her hair was nice. And she was optimistic about her future. I don't know why she broke their rules. I haven't seen or heard from her for a couple of weeks.

# 13 ■ *"One would want people to take the view that the family is so very important"*

# Denise Benjamin and Rena Wilson

D E N I S E   B E N J A M I N

MARCH   24   Leticia's on crack again. I'm very upset. When she was in the drug program, she wrote me a very nice letter. She kept in touch with me and her grand-mother. We had gone to see her December 25 and spent such a lovely time with her. She had even coordinated the fashion show.

I don't understand what happened there, but she left. I saw her last weekend at my mother's house. She did come over. She's lost her weight again. I tried to encourage her to go back into another program. The other day, when I went to Metropolitan Hospital for a job interview, I passed the psychiatry department and they had this brochure. They have different drug programs. So I tried to talk to her about that possibility, and she said she would think about it. But she's definitely on the stuff again.

I keep thinking as long as she visits Hazela, as long as she visits us and we can keep talking with her, maybe she will come around to a program. But I've read some literature, and they say you can't keep preaching to them. So I don't want to be redundant. What I've been trying to do is to make myself a little more knowledgeable about how I can help her. That's the only thing I can do now. But it's such a bad situation out there. It's almost as if people have no consciences anymore. And I try to tell her that. I'm scared for her life.

It's all terribly confusing to me. I mean Leticia has gotten a lot of help since she's been older. I see young people with children today and think they don't have some of the important support systems she's had to raise a child. They may have some family, but the family is weak. It's falling apart. But my mother has been there for Leticia for a long time. For her and her kids. Sometimes I look at my mother and I marvel at her strength. She's got much more than I will ever have. She has given a lot of assistance to Leticia.

And I think I have been there for Leticia lately too. Before she got real bad with drugs, we definitely were communicating better. She wasn't as angry at me as she's been. I felt that, and she said it to me too. Sometimes I do wonder, though, did Leticia get too much support? To the point of someone else taking over her responsibilities? I don't know. I figure you can never have too much help, but maybe sometimes you can. Maybe you just think, someone is going to do the hard things for me—so you don't bother yourself.

It's very hard for me to see Leticia like this. I feel very depressed. Often I think it's my fault. I feel she never had time to grow up because my husband and I were both in trouble so much of her childhood. We had problems we couldn't manage.

**SEPTEMBER 24**     *(six months later)*
Leticia has moved to North Carolina. My son, Vernon, got married, and he asked her if she wanted to drive down and

live with him and his wife. So they've been gone since July 27. He told her, "If you come with us, you've got to get it all together." He let her know that she would have to meet their criteria. That she'd have to be ready when they were ready to leave. That she'd have to contribute some money to their household. But the main stipulation was that the drug business had to go out the window. My son is strict. He really laid it on her.

I hope and pray that she's doing good. She's called me now about five times. From what she's told me, she feels well and is working in a fast-food place. She's gained a lot of her weight back. "Mommy," she said, "when you see me again, I'll look much better. I'm off drugs." I hope that's true, 'cause I really felt what she needed was a detox program.

But maybe being in a new environment will help. I mean drugs are there too. It's everywhere. But I think maybe getting away . . . The pace of life, she said, is slower. And everybody is very friendly there. For some people this New York environment may not be good. I just hope it works out.

And Leticia is a little older now. So maybe she's growing up. She'll be twenty-three this November. Perhaps things are coming clearer to her. She's looking at things a little different. 'Cause sometimes I think she knows deep in the back of her mind that the family's always been there for her. That she's had a lot of support.

But then with Leticia everything is more complicated. The abuse she had as a child . . . I do know that it has had an effect on her. Maybe with all the support she's received, somehow her self-esteem or maybe how she sees herself just isn't—how can I say this?—built up enough. That she just can't keep herself together. She can't overcome.

I wonder sometimes if Leticia felt she never had a childhood. Just the other day I was reading about Sammy Davis, Jr. He said he was never treated like other children. They cast him as a forty-four-year-old midget because he looked old when he was young. He wore long pants when the other kids wore short ones, and he'd just look longingly at them. And I thought, Did Leticia feel like this? Like an old child? Because you know, my husband and I had serious problems when she was young. I was depressed, and he had his own problems. And we had a bad financial situation. We were so poor sometimes that it was difficult to be parents, to be there for our children as perhaps we should have. We were too busy dealing with day-to-day life that we didn't really think about our children. How they were doing in school. What they were wearing. We were so frustrated. Poverty wore us down. In some ways I know I was burned out. Then, when we finally did get counseling, Leticia was already out of the house. So it didn't help her.

And I know Leticia has never forgiven my husband for what he did. Not really. She acts civil to him if she sees him, or if she calls on the phone, she'll say, "Hello, can I speak to Mommy?" That's about it. But she hasn't resolved the abuse he did to her, not in her own mind. She's got a lot of strong feelings about it. And we understand that, so we don't really push the issue. She has talked to him, and he did say he was sorry. I think, though, that this is something that may never be healed within her.

But maybe now, too, her being away from her kids is helpful to her. She calls Hazela and Terry to talk to them, but being with them is something she can't handle right now. She'll say to me, "Mommy, I miss the children." And I can understand that. I know she's afraid they'll forget her. But I tell her that I'm sure they miss her, too, but that maybe this is a time in her life that she really has to focus on herself. I tell her, "Leticia, you need time to regroup, to think about what you need to do for Leticia first." And I think she's coming to grips with that. She has to help herself before she can take care of her children.

But then, to be honest, with Leticia it's sometimes hard to know what to think. You want to assume the best, and I try to build her up and let her know that I'm proud of what she's doing. But will she make it this time? That's what I pray. We've been through a lot with her, and you get your hopes up and then the person has a relapse. I've been reading the literature about addictions, though, and they say relapses do happen. That it doesn't mean that a person will never get themselves together.

But I say this, like I tell her: "I still have confidence in you, Leticia." Yes. You never know what really brings a person back to reality. Those times I talk to her, I always say, "I'm not going to give up on you. I won't do that."

RENA WILSON    **DECEMBER 21**    Leticia came back on Saturday, November 18, three days after her twenty-third birthday. But only for a court hearing. The woman from the Bureau of Child Welfare had written her a letter saying that Hazela had to be recertified for foster care. Each period of care only lasts eighteen months. I wanted to renew it for another year and a half. But Leticia said no. "Only nine months. I'll be able to take care of her possibly by then."

But she arrived in New York at two o'clock in the morning with a dollar twenty-five in her pocket. I mean I'd be petrified to be out on the streets with so little money. When she arrived at my door she was crying and hungry. She said she only had two dollars to spend on the train for food. And that's a long way from North Carolina. About eight hours. She did look good, though. She had gained some weight.

In the morning she saw Hazela. And that child was elated to see her. "Hi, Mommy. That's my Mommy!" she kept saying. Leticia was pleased she remembered her. She couldn't get over how much she'd grown these six months. She did Hazela's hair, and that night they slept together.

On Sunday she called Terrence and asked that his family bring Terry down from the Bronx. When the child walked in the door, all he could say was, "I love you, Mommy. I love

you. When are you and Hazela and me going to be together?" It was heartbreaking. Terry loves his mother. But
Leticia didn't say a thing. I know for a fact that she is going
to have Terry remain with his father and that family. She told
me she doesn't want to regain custody of him. That he's too
hard to handle.

The next day was the hearing. Leticia and I went to court.
Leticia told the judge that in nine months she'd be ready for
Hazela to come down South and live with her. But the judge
did tell her that she would have to get herself affiliated with
a rehab program before the court would even consider giving
her Hazela.

But I tell you the court was a total fiasco, a real zoo. Nobody there really knows what they're doing. One minute they
told me I was supposed to sit there for the hearing. The next
minute they excused me and told me I should go. You would
think they might want to ask me about the situation, but no.
Instead of admitting that they don't know something, they
pretend to know. They make up decisions with very little to
go on. When the judge asked Leticia why she had left the
drug rehab program she was in before, Leticia just said, "It
was too strict." Do you think the judge asked for more details? She didn't.

And the same kind of foolishness happened when I petitioned for more predictability in my visitation hours for Terry.
Terrence's family is supposed to bring the child to my apartment every other weekend at twelve noon. But they show up
whenever they feel like it—one, two, or three o'clock in the
afternoon—so I have to hang around for hours for fear I'll
miss him. But when I tried to bring up this matter at the
foster care hearing, the judge just said, "I don't have the papers in front of me." She wouldn't hear me out. And I know
the BCW worker had sent her my written complaint about
the matter.

The truth is, the system doesn't care about the children

or who's taking care of them. The judges have so many cases, they want to get them over with.

It remains to be seen, though, if Leticia is really going to take Hazela. She's just gone in to a new apartment, and she has a job cooking in some taco restaurant down there. But that only brings in so much money. She is, however, living with some fellow she knew up here, so together I suppose they pay the rent and the bills.

But to me, Leticia doesn't seem as mature as I'd like her to be. Like arriving in New York with a dollar twenty-five. She doesn't think ahead. And I think Leticia has taken some drugs down there. When I called this woman she was temporarily renting from, the woman told me she thought she was on something. That in fact Leticia had stolen something from her home and she had to tell Leticia to find another place to live.

Also, one time when I spoke to Leticia, she sounded incoherent. That slurred speech she had before.

Personally, I feel that Leticia needs a lot of psychological buildup before she can care for a child. She needs to learn how to weigh situations for what they are and aren't. To be realistic. She is still a person who wants what she wants when she wants it. She doesn't stop to think, Is this a good idea? As soon as she got to North Carolina she had a boyfriend. After what she went through up here, how could she start up with someone so quickly?

But I did just receive a letter from her that she got her refrigerator. So maybe if she learns that she's not going to get everything right away, that she has to work toward things systematically, maybe that will help her to face reality. To know what's really real.

And, too, I know her brother helps her—not financially, but he does guide her. She wanted to get an apartment in this dilapidated, drug-infested place, and he talked her out

of it. He helped her to look for another place that was afford-
able. But it shows you what her mentality is. I wouldn't live
in a place like that. You wait a little longer. You work a second job. You educate yourself. This is the only way it's going
to be done.

I hope against hope that Leticia can straighten out her life,
get on an even keel, but frankly, I don't know if I can see it.
Maybe that's because it was so traumatic for me when she
went on drugs a second time. The first time you say, well, a
person made a mistake. But I didn't expect anything like that
again. She was doing so well. I was really very devastated
by it.

What scares me the most about the whole situation,
though, is that Leticia would not give Hazela the proper care
she needs. Leticia seems to take to these ne'er-do-wells. People
who don't seem to afford her anything more than maybe a
good time. But for Hazela to have to live in the midst of this
. . . what would happen to her? And Hazela is the kind of
child who needs patience. I would even go as far as to say
she's hyperactive. She'll need the proper schooling and upbringing. I feel I'm giving this to her now. I wouldn't want
to see Leticia undo what I've tried to give her.

When I think about this whole situation, I feel many things
have worked out terribly. The children have been separated.
Leticia's dropped out of school. And she lost custody of Terry
after all the sweat and tears we went through. It was such a
hard struggle. Yet she didn't have him back six months before she was into drugs again.

And I worry so about Terry. He's six years old, and they
indulge him in a very bad way. He's still drinking out of a
bottle. And when he comes to visit me he doesn't want to
follow any rules. He thinks he can stay up till all hours of the
night watching videos, and when I tell him he has to go to
bed, he tells me he's sick and wants to go back to his other
grandmother.

I'm afraid he's going to be brought up like his father was. Overindulged. There were no rules for that boy either. Letting him and Leticia sleep in the same bed in their house when they were fifteen years old! I feel there's a lack of morality there. A lack of standards.

And I hold Leticia responsible for a lot of this. Certainly giving Terry back to that family. She was the one who took him over and told them to keep him. She could have intervened. She could have told them that she wanted the children to be together. At the very least she could have told the judge she wanted me to have him for some of the holidays. Even when I petitioned to have Terry for two days over Christmas, she didn't back me up. She acted like she didn't know what was going on. "I don't know anything about this," she said, and that was that. Personally, I feel they offered her money to keep him. I remember when she was on drugs, there was some talk of this. And the way she acts with them now, laughing and friendly in court after all they put her through in her getting custody of Terry the first time, something must have gone on there.

It's very upsetting to me. And confusing. Sometimes I wonder if Leticia really wants to take Hazela back or if she's just trying to make the authorities believe she does. I mean maybe like with anybody, it's hard for her to say she doesn't want her children. It's hard for her to say this to herself. But then, on the other hand, maybe she is planning to have Hazela with her. Then what recourse would I have in keeping her? Leticia is the child's mother, and I wouldn't want anybody taking my child away. I couldn't fight her for her own child.

But then how could I be sure Leticia was really taking care of Hazela? I would check out where she was living and if she had a job, but what more could I do?

Sometimes I think I will just sit down with Leticia and talk to her about my legally adopting Hazela. There are benefits I have from my second and third husbands—insurance benefits and veterans' benefits—which Hazela could have.

And I would tell her that. I would say I think it's a bad idea for Hazela to go back with her. Though in the end I know I would need Leticia's consent.

But I do have one concern about adoption. God forbid if anything would happen to me. I'm sixty-six years old. My health is good. But you can walk out of your house and something can just fall on you. And Hazela is only three. She's so young. Who would take care of her if I died?

It's all such a shame. The whole breakup of this family. In the end, the courts are a circus. They give you what they want to. You get what they dole out. Our family's separated. And this white judge, she could care less about what happens to a black family. I don't like to look at things by color, but I think her being white made a difference. You don't expect a judge to be personable, but she was very curt when I asked her about foster care and when I petitioned for more predictable hours for visitation. One would want people to take the view that family life is so very important. That the lack of a close-knit family, the lack of something to hold on to, disorients people. But she doesn't care that these two children are broken up. She's just putting in her day. All she said when I asked for Terry to be back with his sister was, "He's not being abused." But it's not about abuse. It's about *how* children are raised.

# *Epilogue*

On August 17, 1990, my telephone rang. It was Leticia. I had not spoken to her since March 1989, although I knew from her grandmother that she had come back to New York from North Carolina several weeks before she called. I also knew that she had married a man her father's age and was pregnant with her third child.

I was surprised to hear from her. The last time we spoke, she had made it clear that she no longer wanted to talk about her life, that being back on drugs was too painful for her to discuss. So when I picked up the phone and it was Leticia, in her upbeat voice, I was startled, even taken aback. She spoke as if nothing had gone on in her life since we last had contact, since she had broken off our meeting together. I was cautious. For the first time, I felt the way her grandmother acted, sober and low-key. Although I wanted to know what had happened to her over these months, I wasn't sure if I should ask. Would I be invading her privacy? I felt a kind of protectiveness toward her, but also toward myself. I didn't want Leticia to turn away; I didn't want to lose her again.

But Leticia was cheerful, friendly, and "just wanted to say hello." Though she added, in a serious, almost seductive voice, "There are a lot more chapters to the book." She asked me how my family was and told me that she had gotten married and was expecting a baby in October. She was off crack, she said. When I asked her why she thought she had stopped, she simply said, "I'm tired of living a bad life."

Our conversation was short. I congratulated her on her marriage and her pregnancy, about both of which she sounded very pleased. But mainly I was aware that I wanted to get off the phone. I didn't want her to start treating her life like a story again. Somehow her lighthearted tone seemed inappropriate, given the struggles she had just alluded to. I told her I was pleased she had called and that I would phone her soon to see how she was doing.

Over the next six weeks, we spoke from time to time. One of us would call the other to "check in." It was clear she wanted to continue letting me know how she was, specifically how her pregnancy was coming along. During these phone conversations, Leticia complained a great deal about the weight she had gained. She weighed 230 pounds and was very uncomfortable. She was also scared about the health of the fetus. She said that she had been on crack only a week of her pregnancy but had been drinking a lot of beer before she came north. Judging from her anxiety about her baby's well-being, I wondered if she had been on crack more than she cared to admit. However, she was attending a prenatal clinic regularly since she had come back to New York City, and reported that the baby was "at least moving."

The week before Leticia delivered, we spoke every other day. Her husband, Cyril Treves, she said, was as impatient as she was about the birth. He was supportive, giving her nightly back rubs and words of encouragement. Finally the baby was born. Reva (her real name means "jewel"), weighing ten pounds fifteen ounces, was a natural birth. Mother and baby were fine.

Coincidentally, the day before Leticia had called me on her return to New York, my agent had also called, saying that Harcourt Brace Jovanovich was interested in *Before Their Time*. I determined that I would not tell any of the four women about the news until I had something in writing. A month after Reva's birth, the contract arrived and I told them. I also informed them that before the publisher would countersign the contract, I needed their signatures on the release forms. They were all pleased by the news, and I was pleased to tell them that I would now be able to pay them for their time and cooperation.

I continued to telephone Leticia weekly for the month after Reva was born. It wasn't until the baby was five weeks old that we finally met in person again. She came to my apartment for lunch with her husband, Cyril, and their child.

Many things struck me about Leticia that long afternoon we all talked. She looked extremely well. Although she was heavy, she was beginning to lose her maternity weight. Her hair was coiffed and streaked blond, as I had seen it many times in the past. She wore a handsome gray wool tweed sweater and gray wool pants. For the first time since I had known her, she looked like a woman, not a sexy teenager. She was friendly, though somewhat subdued. She was also strikingly nostalgic. She reminisced about the blueberry muffins I had once made, her counselor at the Y, who no longer worked there, the other teenage mothers in the Y program, whom she thought of often and missed. There was a melancholy tone to the way she spoke about these earlier times, a sense of longing and loss. Her sadness was palpable. Although the period at the Y had not been an easy time in her life, it was far more stable than what she had endured as a young child or than her recent, harrowing experiences down South, as she began to describe them.

Leticia had started off well, living with her brother, Vernon, and his new wife in his mother-in-law's home in North Carolina. However, within several months, Leticia's life turned sour. One morning, Vernon's mother-in-law discovered that Leticia had wet her bed, a rare occurrence for Leticia in the past ten years. The woman became irate. "If I had known you do things like this," she said, "I never would have let you live here." She forced Leticia to leave. Although Leticia had been working at a fast-food taco restaurant, she couldn't afford to rent a place herself. She began living in her brother's car. "I slept there. Sometimes I even ate there," she said. "Vernon would bring me my food on a plate as if I were some kind of a puppy. I was like an animal." After a couple of weeks of this, a neighbor found out about Leticia's plight and encouraged her to live with her. "God will do me a favor if I take you in," the woman said. But a few weeks later, a robbery took place in this woman's home. She blamed Leticia, and although Leticia denied committing the theft, the woman kicked her out. This time, with the help of her brother, Leticia found a very small unfurnished apartment for $145 a month. It had no refrigerator. Leticia was grateful for an old queen-size mattress that someone had thrown out. "It beat sleeping in the back of a car," she said.

After several weeks, realizing she couldn't pay for the apartment herself, and missing Cyril, whom she had met in New York months before and who had already told her that he wanted to join her down South, she sent for him. He began working in the same fast-food restaurant, and their two salaries just about covered their expenses. According to both of them, they managed to get by on "a lot of take-out fried chicken and beer."

Not long after they began living together, Leticia's father and his girlfriend arrived on their doorstep. Leticia's father, as he had many times in the past, promised to help his daughter financially. All he wanted in exchange, he said, was a place for him and his new lady friend to live for a while. However, it quickly became evident to Cyril, if not to Leticia, that Leticia's father was on crack and had no money for Leticia. "But I wanted to give him that chance to come through for me," she said. This was not to be, and Leticia finally, though reluctantly, told her father to leave.

At the end of January Leticia had become pregnant, and she and Cyril married. Cyril, hoping to get a better job, decided to return to New York City, while Leticia remained in North Carolina, still fearful of returning to the place where she had failed so many times. "I also enjoyed the slower pace and friendliness of the South," she said. Coincidentally, Rena Wilson was about to reclaim an apartment of hers in Harlem that had been rented out to another family. She offered it to Cyril, who had begun driving a gypsy cab. As Mrs. Wilson told me, "The apartment was extremely cheap, in terrible repair, and located in a very bad neighborhood." But for Cyril it was an opportunity "to make a place for my family."

On March 25, Leticia, two and a half months pregnant, reluctantly came back to New York. "I was so afraid of the drug scene," she said. "Afraid of myself, really. I knew how much I still wanted it." In fact, it took her one week to be out on the streets again. "Some guy asked me for a quarter, and I knew he needed it to get the rest of his drug payment together, so I asked him where I could find the guy who was selling the stuff to him. It was that simple. I just found him and gave him the last forty dollars I had."

Cyril spoke about his own fear of Leticia's drug habit, of his efforts to get her to come home. "I'd be out there every day, looking for her, and when I'd find her on the stuff, I'd tell her to come back. 'You have me now. You don't have to be out there anymore.' But she didn't pay any attention to me."

Leticia, shaking her head, listened to Cyril recount those days. "You just don't know how hard it is to get off that stuff." But her fear that her child would be a "crack baby" finally turned her around. "I knew that I had to get off, but I also knew I could never stay off if I lived in New York City, so I went back down South." For the next four and a half months, Leticia lived in poverty again, working at a Dunkin'

Donuts shop, drinking beer, and barely making ends meet. That August, after much coaxing from Cyril, she returned to New York to be with him. This time, he insisted that she enter a drug rehabilitation program. Terrified she would succumb again, she listened.

At this point in Leticia's life, on the eve of her twenty-fourth birthday, she has three children, all living in different family situations. Terry is with his father; Hazela is with Mrs. Wilson. Leticia has not finished high school but has continued to attend a drug program three days a week. The organization provides her with individual and group counseling, baby-sitting services, and regular medical checkups. When not at the rehab center, she works for her grandmother, helping to care for the five children Mrs. Wilson still takes into her home daily. She earns one hundred dollars a week.

As Leticia speaks about her life, she is visibly unhappy. "I don't want to take drugs again," she says. "I don't want any more loss, not my children, not my home, not my bed." But when I told her I was concerned about how she would spend the money I was going to give her for the book, that it would be extremely upsetting if she used it self-destructively, she simply said, "I've stopped promising people I'm not going to go on drugs anymore."

As their family left my apartment, I had a sad, sinking feeling in my gut. What was going to happen to them? Leticia herself was far from being confident that she wouldn't use drugs again. And she is again making efforts to gain custody of Hazela. How will she fare with such enormous problems? Her sense of self is shaky, and her financial problems are formidable. And what about her children? Hazela has thrived under her grandmother's consistent care. What will happen if the child is again shunted from one home to another, far less stable, one? What will happen to Terry? Here is a child who gets stomachaches every time he has to leave his mother after a visit. And what of the new baby, a child brought into so unstable a home?

Will it be different for Leticia this time? Yes, she has a husband who is helping to support their family. Cyril has found a part-time job as a security guard at a college. But this job is far from financially viable and not what he wants to do. A smart, articulate man, someone who earned some college credits during his two years in the navy, Cyril wants to get his B.A. degree and to become a history teacher. Will he have the money and the perseverance to do so? Although Cyril is obviously intellectually capable of attaining his goals, intelligence is only part of the picture. Cyril, as he told me himself, has a lot in common with Leticia. "I was raised in poverty," he said. "My mother died when I was thirteen, and my older sister helped to raise me. I was also a victim of physical abuse by my father, a man I only saw from time to time. And I was a drug user some years ago." These childhood wounds have continued to fester well into his adulthood. He has been married twice before and has had children, whom he isn't able to support now. Will this marriage be like his two others? And why, at the age of forty plus, has he not found steady work?

Just before they left, Cyril told me that when he was in the navy, he had written poetry. He had brought some of his poems with him, hoping I could use them in the book if they seemed appropriate. I asked him to read them out loud. As he read one he had written to his sister, I realized that I was concerned about the same issues and questions that he attributed to her, although he had written the poem to prove ultimately that she would be wrong in her assessment of him. The poem goes like this:

### Sister M

If you see my brother in the street please give him some
    change.
You see, he's on drugs, and doing bad. Me and the
    family are very sad.
My mother cried just before she died, she feared he

lacks the will to strive. She just knew that once on
his own he would never survive.
So if you see my brother in the street please give him
some change.
He's been married twice, and can't seem to keep a wife
to save his life! Don't know why? Maybe the reason
is he was always high.
I know he's sleeping somewhere in the street, spending all his little bit of money on drugs instead of food.
So if you see my brother in the street please give him
some change.
No, don't bring him home, just let him be; that may
sound cold, but he's forty years old.
He's made his bed, just a matter of time before they
find him in some abandoned building or alleyway
dead.
So if you happen to see my brother in the street just
give him some change.


### Denise Benjamin

When I called Denise Benjamin to schedule our last interview, her mood was upbeat. "What do you think of Buster?"
she asked, referring to Leticia's new baby. Her voice sounded
a great deal more hopeful than it had the last time we had
seen each other, when she wasn't at all sure Leticia would
"overcome" her enormous problems.

We met a few days later. As we sat talking about Denise's
adult life, the fact that she had been married to Reginald Benjamin for almost nineteen years, I found myself thinking about
the long distance this teenage mother had come. When she
was twenty-four, Leticia's age now, Denise had two children
and no husband and was supported by welfare. Now she is
forty-three, and her marriage is in reasonable shape; her third
child, the only one by Reginald Benjamin, is thirteen and in
a school for gifted children; she herself has a job as an EKG

reader and makes $17,000 a year. Her husband has for some time now been a moderately successful musician, a self-taught guitarist who collaborated with other musicians on seven record albums, with one more in the works. How had she pulled her life together? I asked.

In her characteristic way, gliding over the rough spots, she simply said, "I had to." Denise spoke about the kinds of work she has done over the years. "I've worked at so many jobs," she said. "I've been a family day-care worker, a seam-stress—I once made ten outfits for a woman who was taking a cruise—a public health assistant doing vision and hearing screening, a Tupperware salesman, an Avon woman going door to door, a nurse's aide in a nursing home, a baby-sitter. I've done just about everything." Then she went on to say how important she thought her own mother's influence on her has been. "When I think about it now, I realize that my mother has always taught me that work is important. For as long as I can remember, my mother always worked. You could say she has given me a mind-set for that. I was on welfare for several years in my life, when Leticia and Vernon were young, but those were desperate times. Other than that, I have worked, and so has my husband. We have supported ourselves."

Now Denise wants to go back to school. "I'd like to get a college degree. I'm thinking of three possibilities," she says. "Health administration, patient advocacy, or physical therapy. I'm a person who likes people," she adds, "and I want to spend more time working with them directly."

In some way, Denise's goals seem like a dream. She is more disciplined and perhaps has fewer distractions than when she was younger. But her life is still unstable. In the last few months, she and her husband have begun to have renewed financial troubles. Reginald is a diabetic, and his condition is making it increasingly difficult for him to work regularly. "He is trying to get disability from the company he's been work-ing for," Denise said. Although she tries not to show her concern, her stress is evident, especially when she talks about her own poor health. "I have been fighting anemia from a fibroid condition for a number of years. It's a long day for me now. I travel out to Queens five days a week. It takes about an hour and a half each way. Then when I come home I have to make dinner. Things are kind of rough these days. By bedtime, I'm beat."

Denise's family, like her daughter's, is not yet on solid ground. Their financial and health problems loom large. What does seem different now, compared to her years as a young mother, is Denise's sense of herself. "It has taken me many years and a lot of hard times to become more mature," she says. "I have more confidence in myself than I did when I was raising Leticia and Vernon. I know what difficult times are, and I know in the end I've made it through them."

It becomes evident, as Denise Benjamin talks about her life, that two major things have helped her—her religion and the example she says her mother has set. Although she is a less devout churchgoer now, Denise believes in a power "higher than I am." And she believes in prayer, in "asking for help." But she speaks more about her mother. "I want to be an inspiration to my children like my mother has been to me. I have seen my mother raise her family almost single-handedly, during times of great financial and emotional stress. But during all those desperate times, she did her best for her children. She tried to be there for us even when she worked two jobs. She cared about us." As Denise speaks about her mother, there is an undercurrent of sadness about her own life, a recognition that despite her mother's strength and care, unrelenting circumstances existed, which no one could control: their family's poverty, the loss of her father at an early age, her insistent loneliness as a "latchkey child." One hears in Denise's voice both a determination that she will succeed in her next round of struggles and the subtle plea, If only life would get easier.

———

## Rena Wilson

My last interview with Rena Wilson took place in her apartment. As I rang her doorbell, I heard children scampering around inside. Her day was not finished yet. It was almost 8:00 P.M., but she still had charge of one more neighbor's child. The young boy of six and Hazela, now three and a half, were running around more energetically than Mrs. Wilson needed at this hour. Despite her evident fatigue, she was patient with them, settling them in front of the television to get some peace.

Mrs. Wilson seemed more relaxed than usual, perhaps because she has fewer worries now than she has had in a long time. "How did you find Leticia?" she asked immediately. "And what do you think of Reva?" Her tone of voice made it clear that Mrs. Wilson was relieved about Leticia's life. "She's finally in a drug program," she said, a step that Mrs. Wilson had worked hard to accomplish for so many months before Leticia left for North Carolina. She has a husband whom Mrs. Wilson approves of because, as she says, "He is serious and hardworking." And she has brought a new baby into the family, a delight to this great-grandmother. For the first time, I felt I was more sober about Leticia than Mrs. Wilson was. It was she who was ready to believe that things had finally changed and I who was more cautious.

As I looked at this woman, who was now sixty-six years old, I marveled at her resilience. She was still supporting herself, as she had done for most of her life. I thought about her civil service career as a secretary, the pension she now receives from those twenty-five years of service. I thought about the three husbands from whom she had separated, all of whom are now dead: the first, whom she had hardly known but had married to legitimize her older daughter; the second, who was mentally ill; and the third, who became an abusive alcoholic. I also thought about the five or six children she takes in each day as a day-care worker and the sixty-five dollars a day she makes to assure herself of an independent life, one that now includes "cruises to nowhere" and vacations, the theater and dinners out. And, as I discovered, it also includes a new man. "A real surprise," she says. "I never expected to meet someone at my age who's such a gentleman, who's intelligent, who has a sense of humor, and who loves children."

Mrs. Wilson is a woman who has made a life for herself with little assistance from anyone or from any system. Through her sheer determination, intelligence, and energy, she has worked, saved her money, and risen from the poverty she knew as a child. Almost alone, she has raised her daughters. She has taken in her granddaughter in times of crisis and is now raising her great-granddaughter. Her responsibilities continue to be foremost in her mind. As Mrs. Wilson said, "I can rest knowing I did what I am obligated to do."


### Louise Eaton

I saw Mrs. Eaton for the last time at her home in Queens. Although I had told her that my husband and I would stop by for an hour at about eleven in the morning, she had cooked a huge lunch, as she had when I first met her. We dined on her "best china," as she said, but not before she asked my husband to pour a couple of bourbon and ginger ales. We feasted on shrimp, flounder, and chicken, yams and white potatoes, biscuits, broccoli, and salad. Despite her ulcerated leg, for which she had been hospitalized a month earlier, and her cataract, which was "acting up again," she had taken the trouble to feed us lavishly. When I protested at the amount of work this had been for her, she simply said, "I always feed my friends. No one goes hungry in this house!"

As Mrs. Eaton spoke about her adult life, she told me that for the most part she had worked in her home. "I never did like to leave home," she said. "I have always been happiest here." Although she worked as a housekeeper when her children were young, and worked in a dress factory for five years as a young mother, "My real work," she said, smiling, "was taking in children." She used to care for as many as ten youngsters at a time in her six-room home in Queens. "I only charged fifteen dollars a week. I wasn't out to gouge my neighbors." But with this money, along with the money from her second husband's pension and what she still receives from the one or two tenants she takes in, she has paid off her house and continues to support herself.

Like her daughter, Mrs. Eaton is proud that she has never been on welfare. "I have nothing against it," she states, "as long as someone doesn't stay on it for years. But," she adds, "I'm glad neither of my children ever had to go on it."

Now, at eighty-six years old, Mrs. Eaton speaks about her pleasures in life. "I've got my guitar, my Bacardi, and my Jesus!" she exclaims. "God has taken care of me. I have carried out his wishes, been good to people, and He has always rewarded me with his kindness."

From the time I first met this energetic and generous woman, she has downplayed her troubles. She speaks more about her gratitude than of her great struggles. Clearly, she never thought she would get as much as she has received in life, and she never forgets to thank God for her well-being. Her conversation is filled with allusions to God. "He has done it all for me." And in that context she mentions Leticia. "I'm so pleased she has found a good man. He's very kind to her. And now she's in this drug program. I couldn't do much for her besides pray, but God heard my prayers."

Characteristically, Mrs. Eaton speaks of two important goals she still looks forward to achieving. "I want to learn how to play the guitar," she says, laughing, though she is distressed that her leg problems have kept her from going for lessons. "And I want to live to be one hundred and ten years old! I have no intention of dying before that. I'm having too good a time." And indeed, despite her swollen ankles and her diseased leg, which requires daily dressing, she has friends in to play bridge and goes out to dinner with them when they can drive her. And she still speaks about her sexiness, with perhaps a bit less bravado than when I first met her, but still with her naughty, girlish giggle. "Even when I was in the hospital this last time"—she laughs—"the doctors called me sexy. Oh, they know I like men!" And she pointed to the gold necklace "an admirer" had given her, a necklace that reads "Sweetie."

The last thing we spoke about on that warm October day was the manner in which Mrs. Eaton wants to be buried, a subject she had brought up once before with me. "I want to be laid out in my nice white dress, and I don't want hundreds of flowers. No, that's a waste of money," she declared. "That money should go to the poor. All I want is a few pretty flowers on my coffin. Those will be enough."

# *Afterword*

The testimonies of these women—Leticia, Denise, Rena, Louise—cry out for major efforts to reduce teenage pregnancy and childbearing. The four subjects of this book speak poignantly and convincingly about the economic, psychological, and social struggles they faced as children and the tremendous influence these factors had on their becoming adolescent mothers. In myriad ways, their childhoods mirror the lives of thousands of teenagers who become pregnant or choose to become parents before their time. What do their accounts tell us about where policy and program initiatives should focus?

Certainly one of the most significant problems these women attest to is the persistent poverty they endured as children—poverty not as an abstraction but as empty refrigerators, as a child's headaches in school because she had no money for lunch, and as physical fights between sisters over scraps of food. Their poverty—like that of the great majority of teenagers who become parents—resulted in their having little to call their own.

Poverty not only deprived them of the basic necessities of life: food, clothing, and shelter; it rocked the emotional stability of their home lives. It created frustrations and tensions well beyond the normal range of family stress. Living in poor families, they felt the neglect and abandonment that often come when the only parent available is forced to work two jobs, when there is great anxiety over unemployment and fear about where the next meal will come from.

Many recommendations and efforts have been made to improve the lives of poor families: child care for working parents, better health-care benefits, job skills training and job opportunities, and public assistance for families unable to meet the "necessary level of financial support." These have been inadequate to the task. Poor working parents have few places to leave their children, health care for the poor is seriously lacking, and comprehensive job training programs are few and far between. So are jobs with adequate wages. Public assistance benefits are meager and in the last ten years have been seriously cut. Under the Omnibus Budget Reconciliation Act of 1981, for example, the average income that working AFDC (Aid to Families with Dependent Children) parents receive has declined to well below the poverty line.[1] And stipulations still remain that women who marry risk forfeiting AFDC benefits.

Although it is difficult to measure precisely how much poverty contributes to poor children becoming teenage mothers (many adolescents from poor families do *not* become young parents), it is clear that living in poverty strongly adds to many children's feelings of deprivation, disadvantage, degradation; to the need to get out of their homes; to their overall sense of instability. It often exacerbates their fantasies of the perfect family, a family which in their mind cancels out the hardships of their family of origin—"the TV family," as Denise Benjamin calls it, "the husband who works, the wife who stays home with the kids, the nice house." Or even just the family of mother and child. Theirs is a limited fantasy of suc-

cess, in part nurtured by what they have seen around them—
a decreasing incidence of two-parent families, neighbors or
family members out of work or earning scant wages, a general sense of alienation from the mainstream of society. It is
also a fantasy, given their long-standing deprivation, that they
want to enact as soon as possible. These children, frustrated
by their impoverished lives, want that ideal family now, before they become mature enough to care for themselves or a
family, often before they have graduated high school, extended their educations, or learned skills that could prepare
them for a career. In a country in which teenage pregnancy
and parenthood are again on the rise among children between the ages of fifteen and seventeen,[2] a country in which
children under the age of fifteen are five times more likely to
get pregnant than in other industrialized countries with similar rates of sexual activity,[3] immediate efforts must be taken
to stave off this "now" impulse. Part of their ability to wait
will come only when the deprivation level itself decreases and
these children, like more advantaged children, grow up having more overall stability and more for themselves.

These four women describe other grave family problems
they faced that were influential in their becoming teenage
mothers. For instance, a devastating experience that all of them
shared, one that is familiar to a great many poor teenagers
who bear children, is the loss of their father. In the case of
Louise Eaton and Rena Wilson, the abandonment was particularly traumatic. These teenagers were close to their fathers.
They describe them as men from whom they could seek comfort and guidance, men whom they loved and counted on.
Denise Benjamin and Leticia, on the other hand, had little or
no positive contact with their fathers. They were disappointed, saddened, and angry that they did not have fathers
who knew and loved them, who provided models for them.
And Leticia suffered the tremendous additional damage of
her stepfather's sexual abuse.

But the paternal losses, through either abandonment or

mental illness, were compounded by the relationships these daughters had to their mothers. Louise Eaton's mother died when she was three years old. Rena Wilson speaks about her mother's neglect and her beatings. Denise Benjamin, though close to her mother, describes the loneliness she felt as a "latchkey child," the daughter of a woman who, as sole breadwinner, often had to work two jobs and could not be around as much as her child needed her to be. And Leticia was faced with a mother who was depressed, who physically beat her, and who failed to protect her against her stepfather.

These women, by describing their situations, allow us to perceive how girls' relationships to their parents influence their need to leave their homes, to find as parental substitutes men whom they think will help support them, and to have families of their own. "I never had a father to just say 'hi' to or to hug. I never had that physical closeness," Denise says, and adds, "When I first met Charles, I liked him right away. He was capable. I didn't know that kind of man in my life."

They also provide us with insights into how needy they were, how starved for male companionship, attention, and affection, and how angry, how disappointed they were with men and women. We understand how battered their adolescent sense of self-esteem was, how little confidence they had in their future as successful women. They did not see themselves as teenagers who could go on in their educations, who could postpone the need to re-create mother-child bonds until they made something more of their lives as individuals. Perhaps only for Louise Eaton, whose poverty was so extreme that she was forced to leave school in the eighth grade and had no home and no way to support herself, did becoming a mother so young make sense. Hers was a matter of survival. Each of the others had other options as teenagers. Even Leticia, who could have lived with her aunt or her grandmother, might have gone on to finish her education and done more. These were bright young women with the potential for better futures.

Is it unrealistic to imagine that interventions in lives like these can make a difference in how teenagers think about themselves? Is the need to self-destruct, to turn their anger against themselves and others, to repeat family history, so enormous that nothing can be done to help adolescents from troubled homes improve their lives? Although much has to be done to offset such vulnerable senses of self, there is no choice but to try, not only for the future of individuals but for that of society as well.

Certainly the environment that stands the greatest chance of counteracting some of the problems poor, at-risk children face is school. Not the public school system as it has become today, especially in poor neighborhoods: a catalyst for dropping out; a crowded milieu that offers little individual attention to students and few opportunities for teachers to discuss strategies for better teaching and for working with troubled students; an environment in which principals and teachers are drowning in paperwork, where the parent body often has little involvement, and where schools' accountability is frequently lacking.

The deplorable condition of public education in this country has to be addressed. A national resolve to improve education is badly needed when the dropout rate is soaring, when the academic results of our education are well behind those of other industrialized countries, when young people are turning more and more to crime, drugs, and adolescent parenthood. Schools are failing to give teenagers alternatives.

To be sure, school can never be a substitute for the family. However, with increased funding and shared knowledge about what makes for successful education, schools can provide a whole range of critical benefits to all students. We already know, for example, that smaller class size is especially imperative for students at risk, that they prosper more from individual attention to their academic work and to themselves. We know, too, that consistent mentoring programs, peer education, and remedial help improve students' performance and heighten their sense of accomplishment and self-esteem. Students who may receive little attention and guidance in homes besieged by inordinate struggles need opportunities to find role models, to work closely with supportive adults who can inculcate the values of academic success. Many such programs could be instituted during and after school. Instead of padlocking school gates at 3:00 P.M., why not keep them open so that students have a safe place to stay as alternatives to empty homes or the street?

Students also need a school system that stresses the importance of preparing for their futures, schools that offer not only sound academic skills but work opportunities as well. Recently there has been a much greater call for schools to link up with businesses inside and outside their communities, with organizations that are willing to provide not only job-training skills but jobs themselves. Students from poor families in particular need ongoing exposure to work environments. They need to learn the social skills involved in working with people, and the technical skills too. They need to know that they can enter the work force, that not only are they prepared for jobs, but that there are decent jobs available to them, jobs that have ladders they can eventually climb. Programs that focus on career options, however rudimentary, should begin in elementary and junior high schools. Young students must be exposed to work and workplaces through field trips, through opportunities to meet and talk with employees in different professions, and through working in their own schools or neighborhood organizations. More comprehensive apprenticeship programs should be offered in high schools and after graduation. Many countries, including Germany and Japan, already provide such apprenticeships, beginning at eighteen years old.

Children growing up in middle- and upper-class families see success around them. In poor communities, where the rate of unemployment is high, especially among men, where people who find employment often work at menial, dead-end jobs, and where those adults who have become successful move away from their communities, children often have a limited image of what they themselves can become. The sense of powerlessness that often pervades a poor community affects their sense of their own futures.

The United States has no comprehensive policy for educational reform. Those at the policy level rant at the high rate of dropouts, create "czars" to deal with our massive drug problems, and rail at the "irresponsibility" of those who become teenage parents. But they have not attended to or changed a system that is frequently destructive to children's learning and success.

It is noteworthy that these four women recall, even years later, experiences they had in schools—some punitive, some overwhelming, some self-enhancing. Leticia recounts how well she did in one school, where "teachers cared about us, where they had high expectations, and where they went slowly enough so we could learn." Leticia excelled in that school despite what was happening at home. One wonders what an impact education like this would have had on all these women's lives from elementary school through high school, what the accumulation of individual attention, academic skills, and a sense of accomplishment would have had on their developing goals if they had been exposed to high standards and supportive teachers all the way along.

These four women also discuss the fact that they were born into cultures in which early childbearing was common. As Louise Eaton says, "I knew a lot of girls who got married young and had children. It wasn't a bad thing, nothin' unusual." Or as Rena Wilson states, "In those days when you went out with a fellow for a year or two, in our circle of friends, it was taken for granted that eventually you would marry. Most of our classmates got married shortly after they graduated high school. Around eighteen or nineteen, even seventeen." And many, like her, had children very early. Homes for unwed mothers were full, and it was wartime. Marriage and pregnancy were important ways of holding on to your fellow when he went off to the armed services. Twenty years later, in the 1960s, "Marriage was the one big goal," Denise Benjamin says. So was teenage childbearing. By the time Leticia and her peers became teenagers, in the 1980s, "having a child was in." What had changed, however, was the staggering percentage of black children born out of wedlock. This had gone from 42 percent in 1960 to 63 percent in 1970 to 89 percent in 1983. And the trend has prevailed in white populations as well: 7 percent in 1960, 17 percent in 1970, and 39 percent in 1983.[4] It is important to note that although "black and Hispanic teens do not account for the majority of teens who give birth, the differences in the marriage rates for minorities tend to be linked with poverty and lower academic skills for teenage females and unemployment and low wages for black males."[5]

Now, in the 1990s, teenage pregnancy and parenthood are again on the rise, after a twelve-year stabilization period. Teenage boys and girls increasingly see their peers become parents, in and out of wedlock. As we read or hear almost daily in the media, teenage pregnancy has practically become the social norm in poor areas. Teenagers see having a baby as a status symbol, precisely in those milieus where the educational system has prepared them to do little else and where jobs are negligible, and where families cannot make ends meet.

Given the one million teenagers who become pregnant each year in this country,[6] there is a critical need for services and programs that encourage young people to be sexually responsible. There are those who advocate abstinence, but the truth remains that most young people do become sexually active in their teenage years. Although only 5 percent of teenage girls and 17 percent of teenage boys report having intercourse by their fifteenth birthday, 44 percent of girls and 64 percent of boys report being sexually active by the time they reach eighteen.[7] More alarming is the fact that only 40 percent of teenagers report using contraception "sometimes."[8]

Clearly, the availability of contraception and contraceptive services is vital in protecting adolescents from becoming pregnant. For those who engage in sexual intercourse, contraception should be easily accessible in clinics, hospitals, schools, and drugstores. However, contraception itself is far from the answer to young people's becoming pregnant.

Just as teenagers need the benefit of a school system that stimulates them to learn and that encourages them to stay in school in order to prepare for their future, they need help in coping with the period of adolescence itself. This is a life stage of upheaval, of mood swings, of temptation and experimentation, of self-doubt; a time of coping with changing relationships to parents and to friends, with bodily changes, with performance anxiety in school, and with the effects that all these have on adolescents' sense of self. They are besieged by fears of the present and the future. Decision making is influenced by a whole host of factors: peers, families, neighborhoods, and the wider culture—indeed, by the entire prospect of growing up and separating from their families.

Having sex is only one experience about which they are making decisions. Nevertheless, it is one with which they need ongoing and consistent guidance from the earliest ages. With the rate of pregnancy rising among younger and younger children, sex education must begin early, in anticipation of their becoming sexually active. Unfortunately, most sex education in this country is short-term (less than ten hours).[9] It also begins too late. Very few elementary schools tackle the issue at all. Even in junior high school, very little information is given about contraceptive methods, despite the fact that an increasing number of junior high school students are having sexual intercourse.

Some inroads, however few, are being made in regard to pregnancy prevention at the junior high and high school levels. For example, there are now forty-three school-based clinics functioning in the United States.[10] Despite their success, their replication has been slow. The clinics go well beyond the usual inadequate sex education programs. They offer a wide variety of health services to students, including the treatment of minor injuries and illness, diagnostic tests for venereal diseases and sickle cell anemia, immunizations, athletic physicals, alcohol abuse programs, nutrition and weight-loss programs. They also offer family planning services: counseling, referrals to family planning clinics, prescriptions for contraception, and follow-up. Most do on-site pelvic examinations, and several distribute contraception. These services attract both boys and girls, because the range of services is wide. Teenagers feel comfortable going to the clinics because they are highly accessible, more so than community family planning clinics, doctors' offices, or hospitals. They also know that the staff at these clinics are sensitive to the needs of adolescents in particular. At many school-based clinics, students have opportunities to talk with counselors, social workers, and nurses about issues of sexuality and about many of their own pressing psychological concerns.

The number of teenagers getting pregnant shows substantial reduction in clinics like these. In a comparative study of one school-based clinic and one traditional sex education program in Maryland, there was a 22 percent drop in pregnancies in the first program and a 30 percent increase in the second.[11] More comprehensive school-based clinics should be established. So should programs that distribute condoms to those who request them. Although access to condoms in schools is under debate, the Center for Population Options found in a recent study that dispensing condoms neither hastens the onset of sex nor increases sexual activity.

But teenagers should also be encouraged to go to other kinds of family planning organizations. Hospital clinics and community-based clinics are important resources in places where there are no school clinics and during the months that schools are closed.

For those teenagers who do become pregnant, the options of adoption and legal abortion must also be made available. Of the million teenagers who become pregnant each year, about 400,000 choose to have abortions.[12] We as a society must provide these young people with safe, reliable ways of terminating their pregnancies and with counseling to offset unintended repeat pregnancies. We must also provide those adolescent parents who choose to keep their children with services to help them cope: prenatal care, health care for themselves and their children, opportunities to finish their education (including on-site child care), psychological counseling, and parenting skills classes. All these services must be accessible to teenage mothers and fathers in order to bolster the family unit itself. Job skills training and jobs are particularly critical in this regard.

Now, in the 1990s, nothing short of a national resolve is needed to reduce significantly the high incidence of teenage pregnancy and parenthood. We know the hardships common among those who become teenage parents, we are aware of the great struggles for those who become adolescent parents, and we know the costs to our society in terms of human potential and financial expenditures. In 1989, the federal government spent $21.5 billion to support families started by teenagers.[13]

From the personal testimonies of the women in this book, we have learned that tremendous resilience and personal resourcefulness are required for adolescent mothers to turn their lives around. As we have heard, it is possible, but the injury to young mothers and their children repeats itself for years and sometimes for generations. Perhaps it will be the deadly threat of AIDS that finally shakes those at the policy level into sufficient action. With the rate of AIDS increasing steadily among adolescents in the last three years, there is yet another reason to offer children and their families the kinds of alternatives they need to live healthy, productive lives. As Leticia says, "That's what makes it so bad about being intimate. You have to choose between life or death." This is a frightening fact in our times. One can only ask how long both the causes and effects of adolescent pregnancy and parenthood will damage children, families, and society before there is effective political intervention.

# *Notes*

1. William Julius Wilson, *The Truly Disadvantaged* (Chicago: Chicago University Press, 1987), p. 186.

2. *New York Times*, September 24, 1990.

3. National Research Council, *Risking the Future* (Washington: National Academy Press, 1987), p. 1.

4. *The Truly Disadvantaged*, p. 28.

5. Karen Pitman and Gina Adams, *Teenage Pregnancy: An Advocate's Guide to the Numbers* (Washington: Children's Defense Fund, January/March 1988), p. 18.

6. *New York Times*, September 24, 1990.

7. *Risking the Future*, p. 1.

8. Ibid., p. 46.

9. Ibid., p. 144.

10. Ibid., p. 168.

11. Ibid., p. 171.

12. Ibid., p. 261.

13. *New York Times*, September 24, 1990.